FROM A
BARNYARD TO A
SCHOOLYARD

MY JOURNEY AS A
HIGH SCHOOL PRINCIPAL

FROM A
BARNYARD TO A
SCHOOLYARD

MY JOURNEY AS A
HIGH SCHOOL PRINCIPAL

TERRY
CUMMINS

ISBN 978-1-941953-28-0

Printed in the United States of America

Published by
Butler Books
P.O. Box 7311
Louisville, KY 40257
phone: (502) 897-9393
fax: (502) 897-9797
www.butlerbooks.com

To all the students and teachers in all the schools in which I worked and lived. And to all high-school principals everywhere: bless your souls.

CONTENTS

In the beginning, God created the heavens and the earth, and then took a chance when He created animals and humans and schools, or maybe He didn't create schools. Somewhere along the way, He created me, and I liked schools from my beginning. Although schools educated me to an extent, I never learned participles or physics or plane geometry. What I learned was as plain as it could be, but I wish I'd learned more to help me understand what's going on in this world. I do know it's going too fast for me—the Internet and smartphones and transplants.

After my great-grandfather returned from the Civil War, he built the house I was born and raised in. It didn't have electricity, but when they finally wired our house when I was about twelve, it was a miracle, as is all life upon this earth. Although we may be clueless, we have to decide what to do with our lives, including determining what schools are for.

After sixteen years in schoolhouses of various sorts and degrees, my country drafted me to help protect our freedoms to speak, worship, and assemble in schools. In

1956, I entered the US Navy to protect our shores. Then they put us inside classrooms and on rusty ships to teach us how to kill other people, which seemed totally stupid to me. I preferred learning better ways to live a life. After two years during the intense Cold War, I transferred to a schoolhouse to get inside the hearts and minds of the young, and what an adventure that was. I live by what Helen Keller said—life is an adventure or nothing.

This approach to living made a huge difference in my life. Each day inside a school is like no other. Everything I did each day was an adventure. At my advanced age, I wake up, and if I can, land both feet on the floor together. Then wobble a little bit and get on with it.

Let me tell you about an exciting adventure I once had. After protecting our shores for a couple of years, I began working in a small high school, teaching English and coaching sports that required various types of balls. All my students went there to have what they called fun. At first, I fought them, drilled them, and tried to force book knowledge inside them. When that didn't work, I joined them to make school more fun for me, and eventually learned that people learn more when they're not miserable.

With the Creator providing me with strength, energy, and will, I went at educating youth with everything I had. The following is a summary of my adventure in what is referred to as formal education, but you can't do it formally. The only formal thing a high school does is sponsor a prom, where you try to find where students hid bottles of

80-proof. Girls dressed in low-cut gowns sometimes hid pints underneath their skirts for their dates. How could we control that? It challenged our wits, but we had to outsmart them, if we could.

This isn't a biography, but a memoir, which is evolving in reverse, but how could I forget what my teachers and students did to and for me?

When I began my career in education, I began throwing interesting tidbits into boxes that grew into a truck-bed full—things like letters, notes, student themes, teacher complaints, parent excuses explaining why their kids missed school, reasons for being late, disciplinary reports, anything weird, and a few thank-you notes. Twenty-three years after I retired from living in a schoolhouse, I dug this stuff out to write this book. At my age, and after what I went through, I figured I could pursue happiness my way, and write this book any way I wanted to. (I have taken the liberty of changing some of the names.)

As you read this book, think back to your high school days. If you made it through, thank your teachers and thank your principal, who finally agreed to let your hair grow as his fell out. Bless their hearts and mine.

I don't really know why I have the urge to write. When I finish this book, I'll start another one, maybe something about life outside a schoolhouse. Life is an adventure wherever you live it, and what an adventure aging is.

My first classroom—helping my granddad plow a field in 1940.

It's where I wanted to be—in the middle of my wonderful students at Jeffersonville High School in 1974.

CHAPTER I

Lessons from the Barnyard

How could a farm boy, freely roaming the hills, grow up to become a high-school principal inside a stuffy building? Twenty-one years after my first day in school, I became one. Why and how it happened, I do not know. I do know that I didn't want my mother taking me to school that first day. I told her I'd go by myself. After I became a principal, there were times I needed her or someone to hold my hand and say, Don't cry; everything will be all right.

From that first day going it alone, I liked school. Perhaps it's why I chose to live the next fifty-two years in schoolhouses of various types. Our early years and experiences mold and shape us into what we become. My early life formed my character and somehow determined a devotion to a life in education.

I was born at noon on Sunday, July 15, 1934, a day that broke the record for being the hottest day in the state of

Kentucky. I was born and raised in the house my great-grandfather built when he returned from marching to the sea with General Sherman during the Civil War. The house was on a high hill in Pendleton County, Kentucky, halfway between Short Creek and Locust Grove and one hollow south of Hog Ridge, places no longer on the map. Back then, times were bad. We were suffering from the Great Depression and a terrible drought that scorched the land. Nazi Germany had begun rampaging through Europe and another world war loomed. You can't start out life much lower than that.

That's not true; I had a head start, because my family saw to it that I did. They wanted the best for me, and I learned to work on the farm with the animals and crops. When I became a principal, I worked even harder with the students and teachers. I discovered it's much harder working with people than with animals that don't talk back.

I learned a farmer does not succeed if he does not care for all life on his farm, because survival depends on his constant efforts and pride in making all things better. I learned this from my grandfather who raised me, and it carried over to my work in schools.

Family was important in those days, because we relied on relatives to help each other in time of need. My family believed education was very important, and I grew up believing that, too.

To my good fortune, I lived with nature all around me. It seeped inside my soul where it remains to this day. I found satisfaction in going after the horses to harness them for work in the early morn, bringing in the cows for milking at end of the day, or opening the barn door for our sheep on a cold winter day. It was demanding, yet peaceful. Passing by a trickling stream with bird songs and butterflies all around nourishes one's spirit more than a society can do. Later, when I began living in the confines of a schoolhouse, escaping from the complexities and restraints of human nature to God's freeing and sustaining nature renewed my strength to carry on. Wherever I live or whatever I do, country life stays with me.

Not only did I live in and with nature's force, but God himself lived with us, too, most of the time. Every Sunday, morning and night, we'd wear our good clothes to the Short Creek Baptist Church. The Word kept us faithful for another week, but my granddad would get disgusted when things didn't go right in the fields or barns. If a horse balked or our rogue bull tore down a fence to breed with a neighbor's cow, he might say, Damn it to hell. When I became a teacher and then a principal, I encountered some of these very same things with boys and girls. When some balked at quietly sitting in their seats, I tried to refrain from using harsh words.

My grandfather was a good man and a good shepherd. He cared for his land, his place, and all life belonging there. Of all that he cared for, his sheep were special to him. He watched over them, doctored them, and fed them, as he did me. He understood what sweat of the brow meant, and worked harder and longer than most men did. He saw work as his duty, and saw it a duty to teach me to work with him. Those were my first lessons in becoming a man. And so I worked every day except school days from an early age, and I had work to do on school days before and after school. Work on a farm is as never ending as is work in a school, and I was well prepared for the sun-up-to-dark-of-night days.

The photo of me driving the horses while my grandfather guided the plow was taken in 1940 when I was six. Six-year-olds don't drive horses much anymore, because they now work-play with computers, not plows, and few mothers would allow their tender sons get near a horse now.

We milked twenty cows; we pumped and jerked on eighty teats early every morning and late every evening. Pete, our milk truck driver, came early every day to take about sixty gallons of our milk to Cincinnati, forty miles away. City people drank milk from clean bottles. Our cats drank it fresh when I'd squirt a stream directly from a cow's teat into a cat's waiting mouth. We tended more than a hundred sheep, and raised a few hogs for hams, bacon, and sausage that we cured in the smokehouse. We raised acres and acres of hay, tobacco, and corn. We ate from the gardens and orchards, the henhouse, smokehouse, cellar, and dairy barn. We picked gallons of wild blackberries in summer so Mom could make jams, jellies, and hot cobblers during wintertime.

Our barnyard was a busy place with all the animals

scampering about, going from the barn to pasture and returning at night. We had ducks and geese on the pond, chickens searching for a grain or two of corn, and barn martins and sparrows darting in and out to pick loose hayseeds from the ground. I found it satisfying to know God's creatures depended on us. That's what my grandfather taught me at his home-and-farm school. He taught that I could be important if I wanted to be. Wherever you are, caring for all life around you is a lesson that often takes a long time to learn. The main thing my grandfather taught me was to work to make everything better—the land, God's creatures, the family, and the neighbors, too.

It carried over and I believed that improving schools and the learning process would help young people have a better life. I have to admit, though, that I said damn it to hell a few times when the school was more like a barnyard without somebody like my grandfather to settle things down. Eventually, I learned how to calm things down at school to an extent, but there are always those rogue bulls trying to tear down fences.

Perhaps the most valuable lesson I ever learned from my grandfather was that he tried to save every lamb. I remember a day in January, a cold, blustery winter day, during lambing time. When we went over a hill to check our flock, one poor little lamb had not made it. It lay dead and frozen as its mother bleated mournfully, circling around it. My granddad pulled out his well-worn pocketknife and began slicing off the skin of the dead lamb. When finished, he wiped the knife blade on his pants leg and told me to throw the carcass into a hollow, and drive the other sheep to the barn. Reluctantly, I picked up the skinned, dead lamb and slung it to the hollow. Cold blood droplets splattered my face; I wiped the blood on my coat sleeve.

The mother of the dead lamb ran everywhere looking for her lamb, but my grandfather knew what to do. When we got the flock in the barn, he tied the lambskin on the back of an orphan lamb, whose mother would not claim it. I learned as a boy that nature works in strange ways, that life or death is such a chance. It seemed like a miracle. The mother of the dead lamb frantically looking for her lamb smelled the skin on the orphan lamb and claimed it, and let it suckle and live.

My grandfather gave time and care to his weak and frail lambs. In my schools, I gave extra time and care to those students who struggled. The healthy and strong ones can make it without you, although a good shepherd tends all his flock.

I worked every day with our tenant farmers and their children, who lived in two little shacks on the ridges back of our place. They were poor and had little schooling, and some of the adults couldn't read. I didn't realize it at the time, but I spoke three languages, all in English. I spoke country English and town English, and talked to our tenant farm families in—I suppose you'd say—an unschooled language using common words they understood. Country English is plain and simple, and we used words that city people couldn't understand. But city people spoke with what we called big words, because they had more schooling than most country people did. When our kinfolks from town and the preacher came for Sunday dinners, I tried to be careful what I said. I didn't want them to think I was ignorant and laugh at me. To this day, I've not fully learned how to prevent my foot from going into my mouth.

My early work and language experiences helped prepare me for communicating and relating to all socio-economic levels. To empathize with all people, it helps to understand and speak the languages they know and use.

Mechanization didn't come to our hill farm to any extent until after World War II. Electricity didn't come to our house until I was eleven. I remember carrying in a can of kerosene to fill our lamps, and then I remember, like a magic act, pulling a string from the ceiling to get bright light. I remember the marvel of the refrigerator with ice inside. Before refrigerators, most country people kept their butter and milk by sealing it in a tin bucket, tying a rope to it, dropping it down into the cool water of a cistern, and letting nature keep it from spoiling. We kept our lives from spoiling by doing what we had to do.

We farmed the way people had farmed for centuries. Our hands toughened like thick leather, lifting and tugging hayforks, rakes, shovels, axes, hoes, and plow handles. I spent as much or more time with our animals and all the wildlife scattered about than I did with people. The animals were my friends in a way, because I talked to them and they listened when they got to know and trust me. I learned work is more efficient when in harmony with nature's way. I later learned that achievement in school is more effective when taught in natural ways.

Our house sat on a high hill. It was a beautiful place, and we could look down on the rolling hills and green fields surrounded by dense woods with little winding creeks trickling through the hollows. It was my home place, and I still live there today each time I close my eyes and dream. When I was born that hot day, the house was as it had been in 1870, and part of the farm had been in the family for 145 years. A fireplace warmed the living room and a big, wide fireplace and a cook stove warmed the kitchen. Two cisterns on each side of the house provided our water. The outhouse, behind the smokehouse where our cured meat hung, was used mostly by the women and girls. An old Sears and Roebuck catalogue served as toilet paper. Men and boys went wherever they wanted to, in a secluded place with plenty of leaves.

At night, we read and my mother patched clothes by the light of a kerosene lamp. Abraham Lincoln read by the light from a fireplace, and I did that, too. When electric lines were strung through the country to light our home, it certainly made things a lot easier. But it seemed to hurry up our lives when all the modern things came along.

My favorite place on our farm of 444 acres of hills was what we called the Joe Hand place. It was a little ways back—up a ridge and down a sloping hill that had a grove of walnut trees at the top. Our sheep rested there during summer's hottest days. I liked to stop there and look down where Joe Hand, a freed slave, had lived on a little piece of land with his family. A hole in the ground surrounded by rocks was where Joe's cellar had been. A pear tree still grew nearby and bore pears nearly every year. A well near where the cabin once stood still held water. I'd sit there on a rock with the sheep resting under the grove of walnut trees, and think about what Joe Hand's life must have been like. He'd been a slave, and then was freed. I didn't understand it then, but grew to realize that what we learn in life—and school—can free us, too.

As I worked each day on our farm, often alone, I had time to think about my life and what I would do when I grew up. I could drive a team of horses and plow my way through life, immersed in God's nature. Or, I could get an easy job in an office and work with human nature. God's nature doesn't bind, it's naturally designed and free for the taking; whereas human nature, to a great extent, is taught and learned. That's what we do in schools. Maybe there's something about human nature that began to gain a hold on me. In a way, school is like springtime: sow the seeds, cultivate the tender plants, and watch the meadows and gardens bloom.

My grandfather told me about his father. My great-grandfather came to the United States from Germany when he was a boy, and after he married, his wife taught him how to read. Once he learned to read, he wouldn't stop, sometimes reading all through the night. He'd take books to the fields, sit under a shade tree, and read while his seven boys worked the crops. After educating himself, he served in the Kentucky House of Representatives in 1898–99.

I remember thinking I should read more. After a workday, milking the cows, feeding the sheep, and tending the crops, I read some, but I realized it was not enough. And I began wondering how the authors of those books ever learned how or what to write. Maybe someday I would try to write a book. I did about fifty years later, at age sixty-nine, when I wrote my first book about sheep and feeding them. The book is also about caring for all life that is a part of one's life. I haven't completely learned that lesson yet, but I'm working on it.

Whatever my background, I cannot escape the fact that I'm eighty-two now—and still in school. I'm the teacher of my one-room school, and assign homework to myself. If I had a student who shirked his duty as I frequently do, I'd assign him detention or worse. When I get to be near a hundred, I should know more than I do now, as experience is the best teacher.

Among other lessons learned, I've become aware there's a spiritual world out there, too, and it's been there all the time. I learned that the spirit within a school keeps it alive, and I learned that a principal is not a God, but he sets the tone for the spirit inside a school. A lively spirit in an old guy determines whether he thrives and survives.

CHAPTER 2

How Much Education Does A Person Need?

Education was called schooling years ago when I began learning things from books and teachers in what was then called a schoolhouse. It usually had one or more rooms. (My first school had four.) Now, kids go to schools on a campus that might include a swimming pool and a gym that seats a small town. Back then, schooling was also important to an extent. But people could live a happy life without spending years sitting in schools, colleges, and graduate schools. Where I was raised, most people thought they'd been educated after a few years, enough to read a little, write on paper, and add and subtract. They wanted to get on with their lives—work on their farms, marry young, and raise kids to work on their farms until they could own one of their own. Life wasn't complicated back then, but schooling was. Some old-timers thought that too much schooling could mess up your mind.

One could live a good life without thinking too much about developing a philosophy of it. Having enough to live on was enough. Getting too far ahead of your neighbors wasn't worth the trouble. Becoming a doctor, lawyer, or chief of something was too far-fetched. Working in a factory was prison, but working with and in God's nature was about the same as what you'd do in heaven after they let you in based on what you did on earth.

A few of the young people living the country life found something urgent and exciting about learning and knowing more things. And some were like me; we thought about the future, asking, Do I want to smell like cow manure the remainder of my life?

By the time I was six years old, country smells didn't bother me—sweet smells like red clover and rank smells like the hog pen—but the prospect of school excited me. Schooling is broken down into subjects, and there are so many of them; the list goes on and on. Today, kids can pick a subject on the Internet and get credit for it. I studied my lessons by kerosene lamplight until the fifth grade when electricity brought a brighter light (which school is supposed to do).

After watching the old rickety school bus go by our house many times, I dreamed about the day I'd wait down by the road and ride to the Goforth Elementary School. Leonard drove the big, old International bus, and sometimes he'd have to stop, get out, and look under the hood to keep it running. He'd start out early every morning before daybreak over on Hog Ridge, and pick up the kids along the hilltops and down in the hollows. He'd run down Slick Ridge and past the Locust Grove store, the Short Creek Baptist Church, then past Elmer Perry's store, and on to the Goforth School a little ways beyond. Then Leonard stopped and let us out.

Dressed in my new clothes, I carried my new satchel with everything I needed, including my lunch bucket, up the steps and into the school. I was proud and confident, but perhaps a bit too sure of myself, when I walked into the Goforth School that first day. I knew a few of the other kids from church and I knew where my room was, but not my seat. Some of the first graders had their mommies holding their hands, but not me.

I think Miss Bishop knew I was coming, because when I walked in, she called me by name. She pointed to my seat in the back behind where Albert sat. I wasn't scared, but Albert was when he wet his pants soon after we started learning new things. (When I became a principal twenty-one years later, I nearly wet my pants numerous times, not from being scared, but from never having time to go to a restroom.)

If it hadn't been for the Great Depression in the 1930s, I would probably have attended a one-room school. When times were bad, President Roosevelt put people to work building schools and other things. When we'd listen to the president on the battery radio, my grandfather said he saved our farm during the Depression when we had no money to pay the taxes or the loan.

Goforth School had only four teachers. Miss Bishop taught both first and second grades, and each of the other three teachers taught two grades in one room. For example, during the spelling lesson, the teacher would give out words to the fifth grade, and harder words to the sixth grade. Kids could learn both the fifth- and sixth-grade words if they wanted to. The arrangement wasn't bad. A smart kid already knew the sixth-grade lessons a year before he went there.

In those days, many of the teachers were poorly prepared. Some had attended a year in college and passed a test of minimal knowledge. If they knew the basics and a little history, they could get hired. Most teachers meant well, but too many didn't teach well. At Goforth School, Miss Bishop helped me off to a fairly good start. She was kind and gentle, but not necessarily forceful or insistent. Sixty years later, when I published my first book, she came to the book signing. I said, Miss Bishop, you taught me to read and write, and this book is for you in appreciation for giving me a start.

My third- and fourth-grade teacher, Miss Thomas, was all business, no foolishness. She settled me down, put me in my place, and I even learned to write a poem. It was in 1943 and during World War II. I found my poem in 2013 while going through my mother's scrapbooks. The poem was a plea to my classmates to help win the war.

WINNING THE WAR

Are you doing your part in the war?
If you are, then save your money
To buy war bonds, too.
It will help many boys like you.
Write letters to the army boys.
They will enjoy it as much as you do toys.
We want to do all we can
To bring the boys home again.
The boys in the services are fighting each day
While the war workers are working away.
Nearly everyone is doing their part;
We know we should dig down deep in our hearts.

The poem wasn't Walt Whitman, but it did express some of the sentiments of that difficult and frightful time.

When school was out at the end of my fourth-grade year, I remember waking up the next morning, feeling so bad. I was in love with Miss Thomas and didn't know when I would ever see her again. She was young and beautiful, and I missed her desperately and missed my friends. It would be a lonely summer. Each day, before the break of day— my granddad would tell me to go get the horses and hitch them up for work.

When the crops were almost in, I began my fifth- and sixth-grade years with a teacher who was a bit touched in the head. In the teaching profession, mentally disturbed and unstable people somehow creep in.

I'll call her Miss Arbuckle. She thrived on frustration, and when she hit Jimmy in the mouth, cutting his lip with her ring, Jimmy's sturdy mother headed for the school to whip Miss Arbuckle's rear end. They sent Miss Arbuckle away somewhere, resulting in a series of substitutes, fill-ins, and other warm bodies now and then. Somehow, I survived those lost years, and moved on to the seventh- and eighth-grade room, where Mrs. Calhoun did the best she could. She was also the head teacher of the school, but had trouble teaching big, old country boys, who preferred farming and squirrel hunting over book learning and knowing how to spell squirrel. As the words got harder, one day Roscoe, who was almost old enough to fight in the war, had had enough confinement. He jumped up and said, I'm getting the hell out of here. When Mrs. Calhoun blocked the door, he turned and jumped out a window.

Later, Roscoe returned to school and made amends, and he did one of the most wonderful things that ever happened at the Goforth School. After school one day, he took an axe, cut down two long locust posts and hauled them to school on his dad's old truck. Finally, we had the posts for two basketball goals, and made ourselves an outdoor basketball court. It didn't matter that we had to allow for the wind on almost every shot. Basketball was my life, when I wasn't plowing and pulling on cow's teats. I had a goal on our dairy barn and a leaky basketball, and I'd shoot every spare minute I had, dreaming of the cheers to come.

In the eighth grade, I learned something else. A couple of the older eighth-grade boys got the notion to feel a couple of the eighth-grade girls' bodies back in the cloakroom. And the two girls knew how to scream bloody murder and squeal with delight at the same time. I watched our farm animals breed nearly every day, but hadn't thought that much about how people did it, because the church and religious women thought we shouldn't even talk about it.

To become a man faster, I also learned I should start smoking and chewing tobacco, or both. Stanley, who was old enough to be a high school junior, kept a blue inkbottle on his desk, but it never had ink in it, because he kept it as a spittoon. Mrs. Calhoun never called on him, because she knew he didn't have any answers to questions from books, or answers of any kind.

The community rallied around Goforth School once each year. The Halloween party raised a few dollars to supply our school with blackboard erasers, chalk, and a handful of books on a shelf. We'd dress up in costumes our mothers sewed, then parade around, play games, and eat donated candy, pies, and cakes. Then one Monday morning, Mrs. Calhoun called each boy to the combination office-storage room. She asked each of us: Do you know who turned over the two outside toilets? The school had two bathrooms inside, but in dry weather, there was never enough water to flush them. The boys all knew who turned over the toilets every year, but no one ever told her, because of our honor.

During my first eight years in school, I learned to read, write, add, subtract, and spell a slew of words. I learned a little bit of history and some ways to have good health, like brushing your teeth if you had a toothbrush. The smarter kids also learned multiplication, division, and fractions. We didn't need to learn much science or higher math because it wasn't that important, and the teachers didn't know much about it anyway.

I learned a lot at Goforth School, and a couple of things stayed with me. We packed our lunches to school. The landowners' kids always had good things to eat, some of it from the store. The poor sharecropper kids carried a dabbling to eat, maybe a couple of cold biscuits and a small slab of fried meat. We had two sharecropper families living in two shacks back of the ridge on our farm. One year, twelve people lived in a little four-room house. Their kids didn't have enough food, clothes, or shoes to feel good about going to school, although my grandfather encouraged them to go.

And those kids had a hard time learning things from books. Some had moms and dads who couldn't read. They lived by working hard every day, and taught their kids to do the same. I learned from them—something about humility and how to be satisfied with what you have. Tolstoy said that if you wanted an example to follow, you should look among the simple, humble folk.

It's hard to learn in school when you don't have decent clothes and have to walk up a ridge in mud and snow wearing tattered shoes to catch a school bus. And it's hard when you feel you don't fit in. Some kids teased the poor kids, but I felt sorry for them. During my years as a teacher and principal, I did everything I could to make all my students feel like they fit in and belonged. The good students know they belong.

After eight years of elementary school, I was ready and eager to move on up in the educational world. In my case, this meant going to Morgan High School; their teams were known as the Raiders. Their blue-and-gold basketball uniforms were prettier than Joseph's coat of many colors. The library shelf held four rows of books, but the gym must have seated close to 150 fans. And we didn't have to allow for the wind on every shot. It was a dream come true. And what a dream to have cheerleaders screaming for us. They'd holler, twirl, and show their legs. It wasn't considered sinful, but the folks at Short Creek Baptist Church, where I was saved, thought maybe it was.

High school was about as important as our farms were—or maybe not. You can't eat books. Most boys and girls worked before and after school and sometimes missed school when they were needed on the farm, particularly in the spring for planting and in the fall for harvesting tobacco and corn.

Soon after the ninety-nine students of Morgan High

School started school each fall, we'd ask Richard Gulick, our principal, when can we start basketball practice?

He'd say, after I get my tobacco in.

Then we'd say, we'll help you.

And we did.

In addition to being principal, Mr. Gulick coached our basketball team, taught a couple of math courses and farmed. He liked me and helped me as much as he could, and I respected him. (Ten years after I graduated from Morgan High School, he had become the county school superintendent. He hired me as principal of Pendleton County High School, which was a consolidation of two small county high schools.)

I rode a school bus seven miles over a gravel road to the little village of Morgan and its proud school. It sat on a riverbank above the South Licking River, which meandered through a beautiful fertile valley surrounded by rolling hills. One hot spring day, the boys got fidgety sitting in the stuffy classrooms, so we asked our coach-teacher-principal-farmer if we could go swim in the river.

Yes, but be back by bus time, he said.

We stripped down among the trees on the riverbank and splashed around until time to go home and work. Schools don't do things like that anymore.

Academics consisted of all the important subjects— agriculture, home economics, some English, history and government, and a little math and science. The girls took typing while the boys practiced basketball the last period of each day. Our teachers taught whatever subjects they were told to teach, whether they knew anything about the subject or not. Mrs. Winslow was told to teach economics. When I asked, what is the stock market? She said, I don't know. Mr. Gulick taught math and algebra because no other teacher knew much math.

The boys liked agriculture, because that's what we did. We grew the food and the girls cooked it. They learned home economics and typing if they wanted to get a job in town, and a couple of them became teachers.

Ray Hogg was our agriculture teacher, teaching us the scientific methods of farming. He showed us the proper way to do things, like castrating a boar, but most boys knew that from experience. He had fought in World War II and then graduated from the University of Kentucky, and he told us what to expect if we had to go fight or went to college, which I preferred. He set a good example in everything he did and inspired me to make something better out of myself. That's what good teachers do.

(Later I became the principal of Pendleton County High School where Ray Hogg and Lucy Davis taught. Both taught me at MHS, and I explained to them: When you taught me, I did what you told me, but now it's reversed, and you must do what I tell you.)

The boys all belonged to the FFA, Future Farmers of America, and the girls became members of the FHA, Future Homemakers of America. That's all we needed to know to survive: how to grow our food and cook it. But in the back of our minds, the boys also knew we might have to become a member of the future soldiers of America and go fight in the Korean War.

I didn't mind shooting rabbits, squirrels, and pigs at hog-killing time (I do now), but I'd be afraid if something shot back at me. When I was about to graduate from high school, I began thinking more about what I wanted to do with my life. I didn't want to think about it, but realized I had to.

I had three choices: take a chance at getting shot at in the army, work on the farm with few worries, or go to college and major in something. Of about fifty of my close family members, only three had ever attended college.

The day after my nineteen classmates and I awkwardly walked down the aisle in caps and gowns to receive our diplomas, my granddad told me what to do early the next day. He told me to hitch the horses to the wagon, drive it in the barn, clean the cow and sheep shit out of the stalls, and spread it on the tobacco field.

It was the best lesson I'd learned in a long time. Tugging at the manure, I envisioned college professors smoking pipes and explaining what the Greeks and Shakespeare knew. Why not put on clean, college clothes and sit in hallowed halls? In place of pitchforks and plow handles, why not see what books might do for me?

CHAPTER 3

Higher Education Can Be Over Your Head

I had learned to lead farm animals in barns and fields with ivy vines growing all around, but the thought of making the transition to ivy towers was a bit overwhelming.

If high school is higher education, then how much higher is a university? It's a lot higher, so I looked up the word *matriculate*, and in the fall of 1952, was accepted to Transylvania University in Lexington, Kentucky. A minister in my community had suggested that I apply there. Thomas Jefferson had helped establish this first university west of the Alleghenies back in 1780. The minister put in a good word for me, and they offered me a $200 leadership grant. Wow, I thought, they're paying me big money to learn to become a leader of the world on a prestigious college campus in a city.

Just like my first day at Goforth and then Morgan High, I wasn't scared at Transylvania, but I wanted to make sure I fit in with the students from the big high schools in towns, cities, and other states. Transylvania also had a few students from other countries, who spoke a kind of broken English. I did, too, but I didn't want to be looked upon as a country bumpkin, so I wore a sport coat and stiff-collared shirt with a clip-on bow tie that first day to conceal any of my clodhopper ways and lack of astuteness. As I walked across campus to my first class, I noticed the other guys weren't wearing ties, so I jerked my clip-on off. I had too much to learn, but I had to start somewhere.

My four years at Transylvania were wonderful. They had smart professors, who scared me some, especially when I started writing papers for them that didn't make much sense at all. One English professor from England, who had probably read every book ever written, wrote back to me on one of my literary papers: Mr. Cummins, if you are going to submit a paper on the dramatist you refer to as Eurepides, or any literary figure, you should spell his name correctly.

I looked it up and he was right; it was a wake-up call.

Maybe I didn't make sense because I had two goals that divided my attention: make the basketball team and get an education. I went out for the team and made it because the Transylvania Pioneers had more smart students interested in academics than in sports. But if bright literary students in England could play cricket on the fields at Eton, why couldn't I also improve my mind and body at the same time?

I also discovered early on that the males and females on campus developed interests in each other, and messed around, but not necessarily to the detriment of academics. Girls taught me study habits. Some students studied so hard they had to seek relief. Beer seemed to wipe cobwebs from the mind, and sometimes our team played so hard, we sought relief in dark dingy taverns.

When the Pioneers opened the basketball season, I'd made the team, but not the traveling squad. I was disappointed, because the team stayed in hotels and ate in restaurants, which farmers seldom do. After the Christmas break, I made the starting team and the baseball team in the spring. When study at the library called, I usually went to the gym instead to improve my shot. When the grades came out, I found out where the library was and sat there to avoid the dean's list.

Our basketball team was composed of a bunch of wild and crazy characters. We studied how to have a fun time, but a team also learns something about teamwork, sacrifice, and attaining goals. Although a ball going through a net might not be a worthy goal, we developed lasting friendships that endured. All the guys became successful in businesses or professions. About thirty-five years after our days at Transylvania, the teams of the 1950s reassembled and we've continued meeting for dinners, picnics, laughter, and distortions of the truth. It's amazing how a team's win-loss record improves through the years.

We remain a brotherhood, but now only seven members

of the original eighteen are still living. What remains is an enduring bond that has strengthened through the past fifty-five years. It reveals a quality and characteristic of a unique aspect of the human condition—an unbroken connection and fidelity that schools can't teach. We have a plaque with eighteen nameplates on it. When one of the team dies, his name and year of death are recorded. The plaque hangs in the gym—where else?—and when the last one is called to play on the golden court, all our shots will hit nothing but net.

On the academic side, I had to declare a major at Transylvania, and decided on pre-law. Washington and Jefferson were farmers before becoming politicians and then presidents. My first pre-law class was something about the bureaucratic government. I sat there not understanding one thing Dr. Dodd said, but I understood what the letter grade D meant. How about coaching and teaching? Yes, I'll take pre-coaching—and decide what to teach later.

Miss Clarke knew William Shakespeare like you wouldn't believe. She loved him—Wordsworth and Keats, too. She attended our basketball games while her other students studied. She tried to help me; she must have felt sorry for me. I'd sit in her classes and listen to her explain poems about such things as daffodils, ancient mariners, and a Grecian urn. She made Shakespeare seem like he was in the room with us. And I'd wonder, how do those writers put words together like that? To avoid math, science, and everything else, I sat in every English class I could, with the idea that maybe someday I'd try to write something original from my head.

When my $200 leadership grant ran out, Coach C. M. Newton took me to see Dr. Carter, the dean of students. Coaches are always concerned about their players' eligibility and if they have enough to eat.

Dr. Carter—leaning back in his chair with both feet up on the desk—said, come in, but he never moved. He kept both hands behind his head like a pillow; he was either tired, meditating, or simply staring into space as far up as the ceiling went.

Coach pleaded my case.

Dr. Carter, this boy needs a campus job. A drought practically ruined his tobacco crop this year, and the only thing he has to his name is a puny, little heifer calf and five sheep.

The dean slowly rose from his laid-back position, put both feet firmly on the floor, turned toward the coach, looking him squarely in both eyes, and asked, What can that boy do, plow?

President Eisenhower dedicated our new library in 1954, and a basketball player became the night librarian that same year. The librarian trained me to do my job and told me to sit at the main desk and answer any questions. No one asked me any questions, so I sat at the main desk and studied my lessons—an academic salvation.

She also trained me how to lock the library at ten o'clock on the nose. In great detail, she explained how to place the chairs at the tables. She said, I don't want the chairs four inches or three inches from the tables, but two inches.

In working with librarians then and later in my career, I discovered many of them possess unique eccentricities.

Vera Ann Longmire was a smart math-and-physics girl who sat in front of me in a lit class. When she shook out her long blond hair, it would fall down over my book and it affected me like when my basketball shot hit nothing but net. It was springtime with flowers and romantic poems everywhere. How do I love thee, let me count the ways. I gave her roses and sang Tony Bennett's "Because of You" to her. My flesh overtook my brain, and hers, too, to an extent. Human nature is such a strong force that it forced us to marry.

Vera graduated in three years, began graduate school, and taught math at the University of Kentucky across town. She took a math book to our basketball games to relieve her boredom at watching me run up and down the floor. I remember her telling me about a room at UK that had a monstrous computer thing in it. I don't know any more about computers now than I did in 1956.

When I received a bachelor of arts degree, I had a sheepskin to prove it. Back on the farm, we used a sheepskin to cover the metal seat on our mowing machine, which helped prevent sore spots on our rears. Supposedly, my new framed sheepskin would help save my rear in the trying days to come. It did and it didn't, but first, the Cold War.

In those days, all able-bodied men had to protect our

country on this side of the Iron Curtain. One could be deferred to go to college, but faced the draft after graduation. I was accepted to the US Navy's Officer Candidate School, but soon washed out—an utter failure. I attributed it to my lack of preparation in math and science, which stemmed from a pitiful background in those areas during my sixteen years of formal schooling. But there's something to be learned from failure. I could better understand how all failing students felt when they were in over their heads.

In my subsequent work in schools, those students living in poor environments and struggling to hang on were a major concern to me. I gave special effort and encouragement to those ranking near the bottom. Some gave up: why fight it? At graduation ceremonies, I was proud of the valedictorians, but prouder of those who attained success despite conditions that you or I probably would not endure. When I shook their hands, my heart reached all the way to theirs.

But before that, the navy sent me to a ship, a landing ship tank (LST), which is a rough-riding, flat-bottomed boat. Riding in one was like riding a rowboat in a typhoon. You've seen them in the movies: big, wide jaws opening up at the front to let tanks out to kill the enemy on godforsaken beaches. After one month on the ship, and one day at sea searching for Communist submarines, the commander-in-chief ordered me off the ship. The first thing you learn in the military is to obey orders, or they will kill you. He ordered me to go play basketball for the

Amphibious Force of the Atlantic Fleet at the naval base at Little Creek adjacent to Virginia Beach. We'd clean the gym and our barracks during the mornings, and practice basketball during the afternoons, but an athlete needs rest. What better way and place than lying in the sun at Virginia Beach?

After two long years of defending our country during the Suez Crisis, I changed clothes from a little round navy hat to a coat and tie. I'd anxiously waited two long years to teach. Oh, what a difference in young lives I would make.

That first day I told my students the best way to learn English is to diagram a sentence. I put one on the board and explained where the subject, verb, and object went. Frankie raised his hand and said, Mr. Cummins, that's wrong.

I stepped back, looked, and the diagram was wrong. It looked like something a chicken had scratched. I went home and dug out an old grammar book, and learned more from the students than they did from me.

CHAPTER 4

Learning Is Easy; Teaching Isn't

Yes, Tommy, in the back, your hand is up. You say you want to be a truck driver and you're only going to use simple sentences.

Tommy, complex sentences will be important to you to help you read road signs with action verbs and to recognize direct objects in the road ahead.

No, Sammy, there are no indirect objects in the road. Let's go back to our lesson for today, and we'll do a different one tomorrow, building our minds in sequence.

Teaching the parts of speech is very important, because it's in the book that English teachers follow page by page, or some do. Elementary and high school English teachers drill the parts of speech into students' heads for about ten years or more. Few ever learn and remember these things, but devout English teachers are committed to this noble calling, teaching young people how to communicate to prevent human conflict.

An English teacher understands the parts of speech can be combined into whole sentences and paragraphs, which should advance civilization as it enhances an individual's self-worth. I felt this calling deeply. A typical daily lesson might go something like this:

Johnny, tell me what a pronoun is. Oh, you don't know?

Billy, you want to try?

Mary, tell Johnny and Billy what a pronoun is.

Yes, Mary, that's right. Now students, you don't seem to know your pronouns, so we will go back and review them today and tomorrow and next week or until you can pass the pronoun test. Open your books to page thirty-seven and the complex sentence.

Future teachers, be cautious that students don't change the subject on you. If you do, you'll be arguing what a truck driver should know.

After teaching for three days, I was exhausted. I hadn't realized it would be so demanding. If I'd had only one student in each class, we could go at one pace, not thirty-three paces. Teachers are not magicians, but they should know when to speed up, slow down, and when to hit the brakes. They should know what they're doing and why they're doing it. Some never learn that simple lesson. I thought I had until those thirty-three souls stared back at me. Here we are, what you gonna' do to us?

I had read about people thinking they could conquer the world. I only wanted a small part of it, and was more than ready to do it, I thought. After arduous labor on the farm, a bachelor's of arts degree, and two years of disciplined military training, I was chomping at the bit, ready to explode from the starting gate. And I had a wife, a one-year-old daughter and a two-digit bank account. I desperately needed to find a way to feed them.

A coat and tie signifies competence, stature, and authority. I must have tied my tie too tightly that first day. Lesson one: The young can see through a fake. They read people loud and clear. But for what I lacked in knowing what I was doing, I compensated with boundless energy, unlimited enthusiasm, and running in circles if need be. Win basketball games and instill a love of learning in my students—it couldn't be that difficult. They sat there staring at me as if to say, teach us if you think you can.

Flaherty High School was nestled in a solid, little Kentucky community where God kept watch to set us on the straight and narrow as best He could. But I didn't need Him then, I was so full of it—confidence, that is. Did He have confidence in me? I would see.

Flaherty High School and the next-door elementary school had a unique arrangement. The Louisville Archdiocese owned the buildings, but the school was under the auspices of the Meade County, Kentucky, Board of Education. St. Martin Church hovered across a lane, also keeping watch over God's children through the watchful eyes of Father Russell. Essentially, it was a Catholic school with nuns in their stiff, black habits, teaching under a Protestant principal, along with a young, trained Southern Baptist teacher and coach. We operated under the same God, I think. They accepted me warmly and, undoubtedly, prayed for me. Had I began my career in a secular school, I would have had to struggle without prayer. And most young teachers don't begin with a flock of wonderful sisters adopting them. We were family, and I had the advantage of being the only son there, except the Big One.

A few days before the first day of school, Principal Starks explained everything I would need in about two minutes. He said: These are your textbooks and your gradebook. That's all you need, along with a little luck. Remember, your students will lose their textbooks, but don't dare lose your gradebook. It's what a Bible is to a Christian, except you are the god passing judgment. Grade them as God will grade you.

All I had to do was to put names in slots on the gradebook and then add scads of numbers, letters, and checkmarks beside each name to determine brilliance or utter failure, and everything in between. In heaven, it's a simple pass-fail arrangement. That's one reason why teaching is harder than tending the Pearly Gates.

Checkmarks in the gradebook indicated if a student turned in a particular piece of paper each day. I soon discovered I could not handle these stacks of papers, growing like vines in a monsoon jungle. In addition to English grammar, composition, and literature, I taught health and physical education, helped maintain the library, coached sports after school, and swept the gym floor before going home with boxes of homework papers to look at and check. I did about everything except drive a school bus, but in those days, some teachers even did that.

The 1950s were wonderful years. We'd weathered the Great Depression in the '30s and World War II in the '40s. Soldier boys rushed home to wives in bed, and in 1947, maternity wards in hospitals overflowed. With little money during the Depression and all money going to the war effort in the '40s, schools of the 1950s lacked resources and personnel. Most school buildings were fifty to sixty years old, and with the post-war baby boomers, classrooms bulged to the ceilings. And teachers were extremely scarce. I had even been offered teaching jobs without a personal interview.

Vera was busy mothering our baby daughter, and hadn't intended teaching that year, but the superintendent stopped by a week before school opened and said, You have to teach; I have no one else.

As a principal five years later, I couldn't find English, foreign language, math, and science teachers. A couple of years, I opened school with whomever I could find on the street, including preachers and failed insurance agents.

Vera taught math and physics in nearby Meade County High School our first year. She taught one class in a corner of the cafeteria during lunch and kept a study hall dodging errant basketballs in the bleachers of the gym. While waiting for additional classrooms to be completed in the fall, the coach at Meade taught one health class in a school bus. The second-grade teacher at our elementary school had her fifty-two pupils file in, and then scoot the desks together to get them all inside the room. Things began to get better when Kentucky realized that World War II had ended and that we needed to begin fighting a war on ignorance.

I loved teaching and gave it my all, but it can sap you. After teaching two years at FHS, for various reasons, I moved on to greener pastures with a few more greenbacks and two years later, in 1962, I became a high-school principal. Little did I realize that if teaching drained me, a principal position would take the last drop of physical and mental energy from my body and mind. At times, I wondered where my soul went.

In 2011, fifty years after teaching those sixteen-year-olds at FHS, Sara, the president of the class, called and said, We tracked you down, but you probably don't remember me.

Oh, yes, Sara, I remember you; you were the mature one. She was, and asked if I could attend their fiftieth graduation anniversary.

I promised I would be there. She sent information and a photo of the class when they were seniors. There were

Tuffy, Harold, Mary Ann, and Phyllis when they were eighteen. The memories flooded in and I remembered them all. What grand days those were. When I walked into the banquet hall, what a shock it was. They were now around seventy years old, with wrinkles and grey hair galore. A few walked with canes. Amazing what fifty years can do. Had I helped any of them? I did my best, but was it good enough? After the dinner, Sara introduced me to the class:

In the fifty years since our graduation, there have been hundreds of times that a certain teacher crossed my mind, and now I find from conversations, that the same is true for many of you. When we started organizing this reunion, I really wanted to find this teacher so he could hear from us in person how much he positively influenced us. Every time I would write a paper in college or develop a marketing plan for my company, I would say to myself, thank you, Mr. Cummins.

Wow. What do I do? I don't think I can stand up and talk. I don't want to cry like old people sometimes do.

A couple of months later, I met Sara for lunch. She said: We all had stories about Mr. Cummins.

You did what?

We couldn't wait to get our papers back from you, the things you wrote in red along the edge, the punctuation corrections, the tense changes, and the encouragements written in black. We strived to please you.

Sara, I don't remember doing that.

Yes, you did.

Maybe I did better than I thought I did.

Thank you, Sara, thank you.

CHAPTER 5

They Called Me Top Cat

Before becoming a certified principal, I had to get a master's degree. Learned professors at the University of Kentucky thought they taught me how to be a principal, but a normal person can't be taught that. That would be like learning how to farm by reading a book on how to grow food and milk cows. The only way to learn how to be a principal is to jump into the middle of it, and use the trial-and-error method. As the errors mounted, I eventually relied on what common sense I had.

When I became the new principal at Pendleton County High School, the students called me "Top Cat." It was the name of a popular TV cartoon in the 1960s. I liked the name Top Cat, because I viewed it as something like a top dog or a captain of a ship or a ruler of an empire. Teachers called me Mr. C, and as time went on, some called me names unfit for this book.

I couldn't wait to take full charge of my school and make a difference right out of the gate, educating the young, making the world a better place, improving the character and intellect of empty minds and yearning hearts.

I was Moses leading a tribe of wandering children, but not in a dense wilderness like he did. It took him forty years to reach the Promised Land. It should take me only a year or two. But I hadn't anticipated a different type of wilderness where young people grew. In a school wilderness, young people won't stand still like trees do.

Pendleton County in Kentucky is located about halfway between Lexington, Kentucky, and Cincinnati, Ohio. It's a beautiful rural area layered with rolling hills, surrounded by woods, lush pastures, and croplands. Two rivers nestled in two fertile valleys and a number of smaller streams flow through the county to join with the Ohio River to the north. Winding country roads twist around the ridges, which are spaced and dotted with farm homes where my students and their families lived. They strived to make a decent living from the land, but they thrived on living simply and from the bounty of nature's gifts.

My students and their families needed what wide-open spaces provided. They started each day with the sunrise peeking over the taller hills and giving fresh new light, and they ended each day at dusk when work was done. In such a setting, people didn't feel closed in. All a farm family needed was a nearby school, a country store, and a church, and good neighbors to talk with now and then. My students lived this way as I had ten years before. I still live back there to this day in mind, heart, and spirit, but necessity changes our lives and we move on.

Pendleton County High School, established in 1959, was a consolidation of two smaller high schools located at Butler and Morgan, two small villages located on the two branches of the Licking River that flowed through the spacious county. I sat in Morgan High for four years looking out the window thinking about my future. I had two choices—farm and live independently as my own boss or go to college and see where that led. I always liked school, but had never given thought to spending most of my life in one.

Falmouth is the Pendleton County seat. The town had about 2,100 people, with only a few college graduates— doctors, dentists, bankers, teachers, and merchants. The town folks were a little snobbish, and didn't want their Falmouth High School students joining the rural students at PHS, who were learning agriculture, home economics, and basics things from books. Three years later, the town realized our school was on the move, and merged their hundred students into our school.

Although my major work experience had been with farm animals, I felt confident that young innocent boys and girls would be eager to follow me. I had learned, however, that animals had good and bad days, depending upon how they felt at any given time. I also knew it was necessary to keep our animals inside a sturdy fence, which required considerable repair time. As I learned the first week at PHS, on a farm or in a school, animals and students are often indistinguishable. This knowledge was very beneficial to me. It didn't take long to realize that running a farm was similar to running a school. The work was never done, the weather changed frequently, and crops either grew or withered.

On the farm, it was necessary to work closely with God, because He has the final power to pick out places to send storms. When my school needed cultivating, or when my students and teachers acted and reacted as if they were behind bars in a zoo, I turned to the Creator for help, although He never responded directly to me.

There I was on my own. I thought it was *my* school, but it didn't take long to realize it belonged to the students. I worked for them. How many times did I say to a mixed-up student, This is not my school, it's yours? It was built for you, and that's why we're here. I'm not here to make it rough for you. I can help you if you want me to. Why don't you make the most of it and it will pay off like money in the bank.

It dumbfounded them.

When I was named principal of Pendleton County High School in the summer of 1962 at age twenty-seven, I thought I knew the ropes already. Be careful, ropes can hang you. I worked hard that summer getting our school ready to open.

What does a principal do in the summer? Take a three-month vacation? No, he shines the school, searches for and hires teachers, counts textbooks, buys supplies, plans the school-year schedule, and places students, teachers and rooms together for each period of each day. He gets lonely until the waves of humanity descend upon him. If he's not highly organized and ready for his students, they will devour him.

The first day in most schools is an exciting day. Most of the young students, dressed in new school clothes, are eager to see their friends again, and most teachers are eager to impart whatever knowledge they may have and draw a paycheck.

After the first day, the pace picks up. Where is my room, my books, my lunch money? I loaned a lot of lunch money all those years and did without lunch many times, especially when students were in a playful mood, smearing catsup or mustard on one other, or playing other tricks.

By the third day, I started to smell various types of smoke in the restrooms. On the fourth day, a teacher reported that a big boy smarted off to him. Then a girl said that another girl called her a bitch. On the fifth day, teachers and students already knew which students and teachers they didn't like. They had only 180 more days to spend with a teacher they didn't like or a student they wanted to choke.

Teachers make or break principals. Good ones prevent headaches, heartburn, and nerve damage; struggling ones take you to hell with them. Find the best ones. Where? In the early '60s, I hired whomever I could find from wherever.

One year, I couldn't find a sophomore English teacher. Sophomore girls are the silliest; they pursue senior boys who drive cars and park them on lonely roads. Sophomore boys think they're studs, but they're stupid, restless, squirmy, and they'd take boot camp any day before another English class.

After calls everywhere, Thelma Gladden responded. She'd been a Nazarene missionary, loved the Bible, and also loved literature, or so she said. Either something traumatic had happened to her, or she wanted a change in her life. She seemed to breathe okay, so I did not ask other questions. About her third day of teaching, I noticed her students standing with their heads bowed when I'd walk by her room. A parent called. Yes, I'll talk to her about it.

Miss Gladden, I know we want God and Jesus in this room, but I don't think it's a good idea to start each class with long prayers or even short ones. This is a godly community and most of our people are churchgoers, so you can tell your students it's okay to pray at home. Although your students may seem like pagans, you know we're not supposed to establish any kind of religion here.

Miss Gladden moved on after one semester, but then I found Mike Bronson.

Mike was a loud, flamboyant, theater-type guy. He was sharp and a supporter of the make-love-not-war hippie philosophy emerging at that time. He took over the former

Nazarene room by storm. A few days later, I got a call. Yes, I'll talk to him about it.

Mike, this is a godly community, and most of our people are churchgoers, but it's probably not a good idea to tell your students that God is dead. You also know most farmers carry shotguns in their trucks. Mike had claimed that God was dead to generate discussion and argument. We're supposed to teach thinking skills, aren't we?

Mike did make a difference in our school. Our people, as a whole, weren't what you'd call all that cultured in the arts. Western movies in town on a Saturday night and the Grand Ole Opry on radio were about the extent of the fine arts in our community. Mike wanted to produce a play. We didn't have an auditorium, so he cleaned out a large dingy basement room and, remarkably, produced *The Diary of Anne Frank*. The students and community loved it. After one year, Mike moved on to something else.

Desperate for a math teacher, I hired a bright young man who had run out of money pursuing a doctorate in philosophy of mathematics. His name was Ovid, maybe after the Roman author of *Metamorphosis*. I didn't know there was a philosophy of mathematics, but Ovid did well after he overcame his fear of good old country boys who drove pickup trucks splattered with mud and tobacco juice.

After one year, Ovid moved on, as did James, who taught sophomore English one year and later became an academic dean at a university. We also had an excellent science teacher for one year, who moved on to dental school. The good ones had higher callings, but our students definitely benefited from their brief contributions.

A school is only as good as its teachers. With quality teachers, a principal can take coffee breaks and stay out of their way. It was very discouraging to often have to take those who would have been better working with farm animals.

After one year, I thought about going on to something else, too. But what else could I do? The farm called, but I hung up. There's nothing hotter than a hayfield, except maybe the heat in a schoolhouse. No way to stay cool in either place. And you can't study Shakespeare in a hayfield, so we brought Shakespeare to our school.

Although the Bard spoke English, and we spoke a form of English native to Kentucky, we did not speak the same language. A drama troupe directed by Doug Ramey produced Shakespeare in the Park each summer in Louisville during the 1960s. He decided to take his show on the road to high schools, willing to run the risk of having kids throw things at them.

The actors arrived in a discarded school bus along with an old truck full of costumes and sets. From synopses of the plays, our English teachers explained the plot and story of the two plays they would present at our school. Students learned who killed whom and who loved whom. *Julius Caesar* knocked their socks off—there were cheers and a standing O. That night many students returned with their parents to see a production of *Romeo and Juliet*. They loved it. The next year, Ramey and his troupe came back for two more plays and cheers. Ramey told me, Pendleton County is our favorite place to go. Your students amaze me. They amazed me, too.

During that first year, I was asked to make a statement about my purpose, which the yearbook sponsor included in the yearbook, the *Pendleton Echo*. I was photographed in a conservative coat and tie, wearing thick horn-rimmed glasses and looking down at an open book. I made the following amazing statement: The greatest resource of any community is the potential of the youth of that community; our future society will depend on the development of that potential.

That should impress them. I was full of it, but I believed what I said. However, in every school, there is the potential for mere survival or disaster.

Historically, few students in our county went to college, but I began talking it up, spreading the word. Why don't you think about college? Charles and his good buddy, Marvin, were very bright. Charles said he wasn't interested in college; he wanted a job and a car. Marvin wasn't sure. I said, You two might change your mind, so apply somewhere whether you want to or not. They did and Marvin eventually graduated from med school and Charles from Harvard Law School.

Phillip lived at the end of a gravel road where his dad eked out a living on a little farm. At PHS, Phillip concentrated on basketball. We knew he was smart, but didn't realize how much potential he actually had. Thinking and hoping his son might want to go to college, his dad gave him a calf each year to raise and then sell, to help fund his college education.

After graduation, Phillip enrolled in Union College, a small liberal arts school in Appalachia, and went out for the basketball team. His coach advised him to give up basketball and spend more time in the library, which he did. From Union, he went on to the University of Illinois to study chemistry and then to Cal Tech. After becoming chair of the chemistry department at MIT, Phillip Sharp was awarded the Nobel Prize in Medicine in 1993 for discovering split genes.

I said a thousand times: You have more potential than you think you do. I don't remember saying it to obnoxious Joe, but maybe I did. Joe was a total mess—defiant, argumentative—the type you want to hurt. He ranked near the bottom of his class academically and ranked at the very bottom in human-being skills. How he made it through high school, I'll never know. And how he made it through college and became certified to teach, I'll never know. I learned to never give up on any student. Yes, the police took away a few of them. But despite limitations and difficult family and support situations, many went on to be highly successful as mayors, members of school boards, and bankers at institutions where I took out loans.

Up until about the mid-1960s and the Vietnam War

when many groups and institutions in America began questioning authority and the establishments, principals were dictators like Hitler. We couldn't exterminate people, but we could weed them out. Do what I say or you're out of here. Of course that didn't work, because I was a freshman principal, and what do they know?

The two things that undermined the morals of American youth in the mid-1960s were short skirts and long hair. It took a little time for immorality to reach the hills and hollows, but it did like electricity had a few years earlier. The Beatles started it all on the *Ed Sullivan Show*. "Make love, not war" and the hippie movement, with its beads, weed, and ragged clothing, slowly but surely corrupted the innocent young.

Principals met to plan a strategy. Some thought hair should not touch the ears or shirt collar. Short skirts were extremely disruptive. How short should they be to preserve virginity? Some principals insisted a girl's kneecaps should be covered, while others considered one inch above the knees to be permissible. Some principals kept a yardstick in the office to measure skirts. Others assigned the responsibility to a mean, old woman teacher. (Not making any of this up.)

Hippie students said dress and appearance was a free-speech issue and took it all the way to the Supreme Court. The court ruled that schools must permit students to wear black armbands, which some students wore in protest of the war in Vietnam. Thus, hair grew longer, skirts shorter, and a few students at ball games sat in their seats when the national anthem was played. School newspapers printed what principals wanted printed, and the journalism teacher understood what it was. When young journalism teachers began sympathizing with the free-speech movement, stuff began creeping into school papers. Longhaired students opposed school paper censorship and took it all the way to the Supreme Court. The court ruled that schools could not censor everything and had to give students considerable leeway in publishing articles about controversial subjects.

It was a turbulent time with war in Vietnam and a kind of cultural war in society and schools. One day, two of my finest senior boys asked to talk to me.

Mr. C, do you think hair a little bit long is a bad thing?

Not really, I said, and that stupid battle ended.

During my first year as principal in the fall 1962, critical farm work eased once the tobacco, corn, and hay were in the barns. It was a beautiful time of the year and exciting to see our county's young gather at the school. Our students had settled into the routine, exchanging work tools for books and classes. Teachers were happy, enthusiastic, and supportive as I led them, sometimes blindly. All was going quite well until the evening of September 18, when I received two phone calls that changed everything.

After two of our freshmen boys went home from school that day, one hung himself and the other shot himself. The next day was my (our) worst school day ever. Anywhere, and particularly in a school as I learned, anything can happen at any time. But I didn't think this could happen here—especially to the young. There's no way to describe the days afterward—dazed and numb.

Mark was from the northern part of the county and Mike from the south. They had gone to different elementary schools, but we didn't know if they actually knew each other, having been at PHS for only a few weeks. After school that day, Mike rode the bus to an elementary school and played basketball while waiting to catch another bus home. After arriving home, he went out to a shed and hanged himself.

Mark rode his bus home and shortly thereafter took a gun with him to go bring their cows in to milk. When he didn't return, his father went looking for him, and found him dead, lying in a field with the gun nearby.

There were rumors in the community that the two had signed a suicide pact. Mark's family wanted to believe he'd stumbled or something, and that the gunshot was an accident.

When I removed their belongings from their lockers, I found a sketch Mike had drawn in his notebook of the shed where he took his life. Mark went after the cows as he always did, with his gun. (It was not unusual then for farm boys to carry guns on farms to shoot varmints and such.) Both families and friends were unaware of any problems or concerns, and both boys seemed normal and happy. All going well until, suddenly, two young boys with promising futures vanished forever.

What could I say to the parents, the students, and teachers? The next day after a totally numbing day at school, our staff met. It was the saddest of times, a collective semi-paralyzed daze and only a few had dry eyes. I said, I don't want you to feel that we contributed to this in any way, but we must always try to be aware of the severest problems of all our students.

From that time on, we remained ever aware of the feel for and insight necessary to protect our young. Call it a primary responsibility or another burden; it was both. There would be other student suicides, untimely deaths by natural causes, and accidental deaths, most often in car accidents. When committing to the education and welfare of the young, a loss of one child leaves a scar never to be completely healed. Without explanation, what can be said other than, We must carry on.

We (I) made it through the year. Graduation time— good luck, good-bye, and thank God. They marched in, tassels swaying, flashbulbs, parents with silly grins. Bobby was the last in line, but he had no chair. Can't the custodians count? Somebody, please find a chair for Bobby to sit on so he can hear the commencement address, probably something about potential. Bobby found a seat, and they all marched out with diplomas in hand. What a relief!

The next day, I sat in my office cooling down and the phone rang. I received calls day and night, calls from cranks, concerned mothers crying and irate fathers cussin'. What kind of damn school you runnin' over there? Most people are nice after they cool down.

Hello. Yes, I'm the principal.

Just wanted to tell you thanks for helping my son get through school.

Thank you very much.

CHAPTER 6

To Paddle or Not to Paddle: That Is the Question

With 490 students, not enough teachers, one secretary, and no counselors, assistants, or aides, I did everything from taking ill or injured students to the doctor to mopping up vomit when the janitors disappeared. When Connie, a silly sophomore, stopped breathing, or nearly did, I rushed her to the doctor. When he said, get calm, she did and lived. I rushed back to school to see what happened while we were away. I learned to take it as it comes. Sometimes, it was like rain when it floods and the roof leaks. That's when you mop up.

One important thing, though, I eventually learned the names of every student. It helps. A principal knows the names of the student leaders, honor students, and athletes. The problem ones and the ones with problems began appearing in my office on the third day, with or without notes of explanation. I got to know them intimately.

Why are you here, Jimmy?

I was just sitting there, doing nothing, and she sent me here for nothing.

Sometimes, it's better to do nothing than to do something, like throwing things, making weird noises, tapping on the desk, or poking Suzy. Students think of creative ways to disrupt the learning process in a classroom. Drowsy students don't disrupt when their heads slump to a desk. Why fight it? Don't wake them.

As the years went by, teachers became a bit more lax as students became less disciplined at home and elsewhere for whatever reasons. When I went to school in the 1940s and '50s, the teachers ruled. Get a paddling at school and you got one at home. An all-powerful principal could not maim a body, but he could paddle a behind, which I did my first couple of years. It wasn't in my nature, but I assumed I had to do things the traditional way. I knew principals who kept a paddle hanging on the wall behind their desk. Fearing the principal is conducive to an orderly school and a pleasant atmosphere—or maybe not.

How to correct a disruptive or misbehaving student? Talk to, warn, punish, suspend, or expel them? Talking with them worked the best, but I never had enough time when we operated with a bare-bones staff. Rendering punishment was the quick and easy way. What punishment? I don't know: stand them in the corner or order them to write "I will behave myself" or something else ridiculous 500 times. It took years of experience and cultural change to learn better ways to alter their behavior.

I paddled back then, but it bothered me. When my words of wisdom had no effect or my patience ran out, it was three licks.

You're not paddling me, the big old country boy said.

Then you're outta' here, I said.

Suspension doesn't solve many problems either. I gave them an option: three licks or three days. One senior boy took the licks. He said that if he was sent home for three days, his dad would take away his car keys.

Paddling is quick, efficient, and saves time. What about the girls? Some schools had a mean old female teacher who took pleasure in paddling girls. In a neighboring school, when a boy went home with bruises on his rear, a lawsuit ended corporal punishment in that neighborhood. We weren't exactly barbarians fifty-five years ago, but that's the way it was. Traditions are as difficult to break in schools as in the larger society.

Randy, the last student I paddled, was a stinker—not malicious, just excessively mischievous.

I've had enough out of you, I said. Empty your pockets and bend over with both elbows on my desk.

Drawing the paddle back, I paused.

Randy, what would your mother think of the way you've been behaving?

My mother's dead, he said.

Hesitating, I asked, Well then what would your dad think?

My dad's dead, too.

I later learned they were. I lightly tapped three times on his rear, and he was the last human being I ever physically assaulted. I learned that, in a way, I had to assault their minds, their disadvantages, and their feelings to win them over.

I was so busy, I almost forgot I had a family. I saw them at Thanksgiving, Christmas, and on Sundays. I loved my wife, Vera, who bore our four children in only four years, four months. When not bearing children, she taught math and physics, and was a whiz at it. We had twins last and enough was enough. When I became a principal in 1962, Alice Danette (Dani) was six; Timothy (Tim) was three; and twins John Clinton (Clint) and Paul Curtis (Curt) were two. Little Tim called Clint and Curt Dent and Dirt. After an exhausting day at school, I went home and washed a huge bucket of diapers dirtied by the three boys. (Disposable diapers weren't available until much later.)

When the boys became about five, I'd take them to school during the summer and let them play while I worked in the office. One day, janitors Frank and Willard rushed in alarmed. A skunk had fallen into a five-foot-deep window well near the gym.

Don't worry Frank. I have a college education and know

how to solve problems. Put a long pole down in the window well and the skunk will climb out tonight.

The next day, Clint and Curt went exploring. They came running excitedly to my office with a cardboard box tied with string. Setting the box by my desk, they said, We captured it, Dad.

How they put the skunk in the box, and why it didn't use its chemical weapon, I'll never know. God works in mysterious ways.

God really works in mysterious ways in schools. He has these chosen people—children—which He likes more than those leading them. Jesus said unto them, Come unto me. I said, Do not come unto me. Stay in your classroom, but they didn't. They were sent in for me to judge.

What happens in the classroom is what matters. Traditionally, it's dull and boring—the same old thing, or at least much of it was and is.

Open your books and Mary, you read the first paragraph; Marty, you read the second one; and on and on until the bell rings. In math, Mary, you put the first problem on the board; Marty, you do the second one; and on and on until the bell rings.

Going through the motions to where? Too many time-killing things occur in many schools. Why not make our school come alive? Innovate, create, and try some new and different things. Perhaps I lacked competence, but not enthusiasm. I believed learning is, or can be, interesting, even exciting.

Our teachers were conscientious and felt the same way, so we began to move out of the same old rut. Our geography teacher got the bright idea of studying the geography of Kentucky from the sky. We contacted an airlines at the Cincinnati airport, and with an opportunity for some good publicity, they charged a discounted rate. With excitement mixed with apprehension, about fifty students, teachers, and I boarded the plane.

A professor of geography described the geological formations of Kentucky as we flew over the commonwealth. More than half of the young passengers had never flown before, and when we flew into some mild turbulence, several stomachs began churning. As any dedicated principal would do, I helped the flight attendant distribute barf bags to them. When we touched down and boarded the bus back to the hills of home, it was a good feeling knowing that our adventure somehow brought us a little closer together.

Ask anyone, What's the best meal you ever had? The question piques interest and great responses. One of the best meals I ever had was served in a PHS home-economics classroom. Each year for a week, our agriculture teachers traded students with the home-economics teachers. The boys learned to cook, clean, and how to change diapers. The girls learned about soil, tractors, and how to butcher hogs.

Mr. C. you're invited to lunch.

The night before, the boys went frog hunting in

surrounding farm ponds. With fresh salads from the gardens, cornbread, baked beans, home-fried potatoes, and a huge platter of crispy, fried frog legs, it was a meal you could not buy in a fancy restaurant. The strawberry pie topped off with fresh whipped cream from Billy's dairy herd sent me back to the office needing a snooze, but Elza was waiting for me.

He handed me a note from Miss Clark: Elza said "damn it" when I woke him up.

Elza, did you say that?

To be honest, yes I did.

Well, to be honest with you, why in the hell did you say that? (No, I didn't respond like that. Back in those proper days, teachers and principals didn't cuss.)

After one student left my office, there was usually another one waiting.

Come on in, Freddy. What is it now?

Mr. Brown sent me here.

Why?

Aw, Mr. C, I guess because I can't get interested in history or anything else in school.

Yes, he told me you wouldn't do anything but sit there. I've talked to you before about this, and here we go again. Let's talk about you and your future, not me or mine.

To break the ice, we talked farming and fishing, leading up to the chapter on the Civil War in his history class and on to his life in school, and how that would lead to what he hoped his life would be, topped off with how to get there. I gave this type of sermon thousands of times, and eventually got it down pat.

Do you want to dig ditches or graves to make a living, or would you rather have a beautiful farm with a beautiful wife and kids? You see, it's up to you, not me, but I want to see you live up to your capabilities, which are more than you realize. I'll be proud of you if you do.

He did say that he had buddies fighting in the Vietnam War, and that he might as well go on and get himself killed and get it over with.

He sat there fidgeting, squirming and staring with that beat-puppy look on his face.

To warm him up, I asked, Who's your favorite teacher and class?

I reckon Mr. Hogg and agriculture, he said.

Freddy perked up when I told him Mr. Hogg taught me ten years earlier and was one of my favorite teachers, too.

Mrs. Lucy Davis, across the hall from your history class was also another favorite teacher of mine. She taught me back during the Korean War. She had also taught one of the marines who helped raise the flag on Iwo Jima, and he didn't return home. If you pass history, Freddy, you will take government from her next year and I hope you do.

I remember she used to stand in front of our class and tell us about how Franklin Roosevelt saved us during World War II and what the other presidents did. I also remember her saying the army discovered that eighteen-year-olds make the best soldiers, because they're not afraid.

She wasn't talking about me, because I was near eighteen then, and I was afraid of getting killed. But as Freddy said earlier, he had buddies fighting in the Vietnam War and couldn't make himself do anything in school, so he might as well go ahead to the war, get himself killed and get it over with.

Look Freddy, you know we all have to do things we'd rather not do in order for better days to come. Think about getting your diploma next year, having money in your pocket, and then a few years later, taking your boy squirrel hunting with you. Take a history book to class, stay awake, and try to remember a few answers to the tests. You should thank Mr. Brown for teaching you the Civil War, so we don't keep repeating our past mistakes. Will you do it?

Aw, Mr. C, I can't get my mind on history, because, you know, I think it's sorta out of date.

The next year, I presented Freddy with a diploma and shook his hand, and always remembered what he said, that history is sorta out of date. He's right in a way, but I must continue on and not repeat my past mistakes.

After my first year leading youth, I decided to evaluate myself as all Top Cats should do. In the quiet of my office with the only sound coming from my janitors, Frank and Willard, who were scrubbing down the inside of our building, I jotted down some of the things I encountered during my first year. It was lonely in the school that summer and sometimes a principal feels as if he has no friends, except perhaps his janitors. Frank and Willard were loyal workers, but more importantly, they kept me informed of the strange things occurring in the dark corners of our school. One day, Willard rushed in to report that a boy and a girl were doing something in the storage room where they kept their cleaner and rags.

As I began jotting down the things I had to do, I thought, my God, I didn't realize being top dog would be like this. The first thing that crossed my mind was the big yellow buses that delivered the kids to me each day. I often wished to be delivered from them, and this is why:

The people who drive the big yellow buses
The people who should not drive the big yellow buses
The people riding in the back seats of the big yellow buses
Six packs in the cars in the parking lot
School board members who shouldn't be school board members
People in the central office who shouldn't be in any office
Parents who only think they're parents
Stepparents, foster parents, Grandma, Mom's boyfriend
Teacher anxiety, illnesses, breakdowns
Substitute teachers (it's a zoo in there)
Balanced lunches, food fights
Proms where strong drink is concealed under the girls' strapless gowns

Rock bands, sock hops, shaking it

Playing, joking, messing around, coming on, backing off

Stability, instability, anxiety, stress. You feel sick? I do, too.

Diagnosis, counseling, medication, passing out, passing gas

Fluids, spit, vomit, mucus, blood; no, not tears again

Spitballs, peashooters, squirt guns, smoke bombs, spray paint

Tobacco, alcohol, drugs, glue, paint thinner, weapons; he's chewing gum again

Headlocks, fisticuffs, discipline, punishment, suspensions, expulsions

No school spirit, too much school spirit, idiots in the bleachers

Pep rallies, ball games, concerts, contests

Cheerleaders, pom-poms girls, homecoming queens, unwed mothers

Sex education, uneducated sex, unwanted sex

Spiritualism and heathenism

Evangelicalism; let us pray; it's not legal

Profanity, vulgarity, hate mail, sentence fragments

The Constitution guarantees free speech; no, it doesn't; shut your mouth

Absenteeism, absentmindedness, feeblemindedness, tardiness, runaways

You missed the bus. Huh, what else are you missing?

The curriculum needs developing and so do you
Boredom is better than bedlam
Teach beatitudes to those with bad attitudes
Grading, testing, evaluation, achievement, accountability
The teacher failed your son and so did you
Jocks, preps, bullies, bitches, hoods, jerks, teacher's pets
Student dress codes, speech codes, the F-word code
Innovation, change, reluctance to change anything
The way we did it before you came
You broke a rule; you get off my back
Seniors, restless, anxious, rebellious
Juniors who think they're seniors
Sophomores, the lowest form of humankind
Freshmen, God help them

This is only a partial list of what I did. But how did the education process go? I don't have a clue.

Looking back on that year, and all my years in schools, I remember the good days most—the successes, the excitement of the teaching-learning process, and the bountiful youthful exuberance and energy. And if that doesn't rub off on the principal, he's dead. There's no way to survive without giving it your all and then reaching back for more.

Amidst occasional tears, all the smiley and funny faces and the fun and laughter kept me there.

CHAPTER 7

That's Not a Good Excuse

Food on the table is more important than a cap and gown. Farm boys go to school when the crops are in. They don't go that often, because the crops are never completely in, the cows get out, or it looks like rain and the hay will get wet. We stressed attendance, attendance, attendance!

We told them, If you don't attend school you'll do slave labor forever. But if you miss school, you must bring a note of explanation from a parent.

And teachers, remember, don't admit a student who has been absent in your class unless he has a certified admittance pass from the principal. And don't forget, you cannot teach if you're not here. Unless you are hospitalized, show up.

Each morning, I sat in my office signing notes from parents explaining why their child was absent. Parents in our community wanted their children in school, but if they were needed at home to work, that took priority. There were other legitimate excuses, too, such as when a creek rose over its banks.

Children learn to make excuses at a very early age. I don't feel good. What's wrong? Stomach, head, side hurts, funny feeling. Why don't you stay home? It might pass. But you won't pass if you don't go to class.

When I read the excuse notes, I tossed the gems in a file, which eventually grew into a drawer full. There are excuses and then there are good excuses. Be honest about it; just say Ernie was absent because he doesn't like school.

A sharp principal learns to decipher handwriting and recognize forgeries. The following excuses were written by parents, or students, or a girlfriend, or a sympathetic grandma.

Dear Sir, I had to take Laymon to register yesterday. He went to the wrong place and registered to vote. He didn't know I wanted him to register for the army.

The reason Dale was absent was I taken him with me to the Tax Commissioner and Equalization Board. I thought it might be of use to him someday.

Foster had to go see a man from Detroit to fix his new tractor which they have tride 4 times before.

Glenda is late because she missed the bus. Up here in the woods where we live, you can't see the bus.

Jim missed the school bus. There has been a home remodeled across from us and have installed electric heat, and since they moved in we have nothing but electricity trouble.

Larry was absent yesterday because we had to go decide what to do about a man that shot at our boys for putting a pumpkin in the road on Halloween.

Lee was absent because he had to go get his driver's permit. His father had an eye put out in '57 and he cant drive too good since.

Jimmy was absent yesterday because our tobacco got hot. (After tobacco dries in the rafters of a barn, it is taken down and put in piles in preparation for stripping the leaves from the stalks. Then it's tied in bundles and sent to market. If the tobacco is not completely dried, it heats and rots. It's like putting money in a pile and setting fire to it.)

I was absent Wednesday because I got married. We went on a little honeymoon.

Peggy missed school yesterday because there wasn't a bite to eat in the house.

Suzy missed school because nothing would lay on her stomach.

We took Marie to the doctor yesterday to see if she was pregnant.

Please excuse Charles. We live near the river. He was watching the water for us.

Excuse Sue for Friday, because she could not get across the creek.

Roger was home Friday because his shoes tore up.

Bobby had to work yesterday and get the cemetery moved.

Brenda has no blood and is under doctor's care.

Raymond had to dig a ditch.

Jack got off the bus yesterday morning to help his stepfather out of a ditch.

Jake has come home and said he was expelled from school and I want to know the reason why? I am sending him back to school and he had better stay over there. If there is any fist work, you can do it with me. His stepfather

I certainly did not want to conduct fist work with Jake's stepfather. All I wanted was for these young people to come to school, and grow, learn, and be better prepared to overcome adversity. But the human condition gets all tangled up at times. One reason the world doesn't work as it should or could is there's always an excuse for it.

Other authentic excuse notes:

Donna had a slight heart attack.

Mike went to the dentist and trouble set in.

Alice has neuralgia in her teeth.

Brenda's glands and liver hurt her.

Jack's pants ripped.

Kenny had poison oak.

Bruce stayed home to get the cows off the road.

Otis was home hauling rocks and two of our tires went flat.

Roy had the runs.

John stepped in a groundhog hole.

Brenda's muscles and leaders in her neck are all in a bunch.

Dr. Rice of Covington, Kentucky, certified that Caroline was here today for head trouble.

Yes, head troubles are a problem, mine included. Maybe I should go see Dr. Rice, because I don't feel like going to school today. No, I will go no matter what. The school could not function without me, could it?

I also received notes from parents such as the one Mrs. Johnson sent: Mr. Cummins, I had to have the boys to help me so they could have something to go to school on. I will not keep them out any more if I can. And I will have you some money sometime next week on the books. I will do all I can, will see you get every penny.

In families where every penny counts, those of us counting hundred-dollar bills often don't realize the difficulties those families endure. I needed to work out some kind of deal with families like Mrs. Johnson's. It was one more thing for me to think about and do, but it would pay off if and when they walked through the line at graduation.

The first responsibility of a principal is to keep all students safe from harm. A storm can blow in even on a good day. In the early spring of 1964, it rained and rained some more. The creeks rose and then the water rose in the town of Falmouth between the two rivers in the valley below our school. Six feet of water in half of the town drove the people out.

My family lived on a hill above the valley a half mile across from the school. Twenty-seven women and children stayed in our home for two days and nights. I opened the school for other refugees and stayed there with them. After the water receded, the community spent several days cleaning up and drying out before school resumed.

Four years later, in the spring of 1968, disaster struck again. I'll never forget the expression on Steve's face. It was a blustery day, but nothing unusual and no weather warnings. Steve was in my wife's physics class when they spotted a funnel cloud touching down about a mile from our school. (Vera had returned to teaching when our twins were about four. I was her boss at school, but the roles reversed when we went home.)

Steve burst into my office shouting, Come quick, there's a tornado on the way.

I ran to that part of the building, looked out the window, and there it was, headed toward our school. It turned eerily dark as I ran back to the office to announce on the intercom that everyone should go to the basement in the gym. By that time, students were already out in the hallway after hearing the roar of the wind and the softball-size hailstones hitting the roof and breaking the plastic skylight domes. The plastic pieces shattered (not glass, thank God) and fell on the screaming, panicked students—then suddenly, all was quiet.

The tornado missed our school by about a half-mile,

but twisted through the nearby river valley taking out the half of Falmouth that the flood didn't destroy four years earlier. Miraculously, only four people lost their lives. In a graveyard one block from the Falmouth Elementary School, the tornado lifted tombstones from the ground, but only slightly damaged the school.

After the shock and devastation, we dismissed school for several days. The community rallied to pick up the pieces and move on. Steve's physics class researched tornadoes for a couple of weeks, and learned more about tornados than many weather forecasters know. It took time, but our strong community—with everyone pitching in—bounced back amazingly well.

The death of a young person is particularly traumatic. Farm boys and many farm girls learn to drive tractors and trucks at a very early age. Future Farmers of America members raise crops and livestock, and by the time they're sixteen, they have enough money to buy a sleek, souped-up car. The problem is, they drive like maniacs. Warn them, preach to them, but it doesn't seem to get through. During one twelve-month period, eight of our students were killed in car wrecks. The worst of all occurred a few years later. Three senior girls and one senior boy got in a car after school and ten minutes later hit a dump truck head on. All were killed instantly. An hour or so before the accident, one of the senior girls had written in her notebook: I hope I never have to come back to this school.

Deaths of classmates are devastating, but most young people are resilient. I repeatedly announced—whatever you do, drive carefully. I observed that after a death, student drivers slowed down for a month or two. But what is it about human behavior—young or old—that we never learn?

Each year, I made numerous visits to funeral homes and attended the funerals of several of our young people. Car accidents took a huge toll, but others died from cancer, heart disease, and other illnesses and accidents. These tragedies shouldn't happen to the young, but they do, and their deaths take a numbing toll. And when a young person takes his or her own life, the nagging and unexplainable questions remain. The signs are undistinguishable, the pain unfathomable, and the grief will not go away.

We were all in it together, as the school is a family in many ways. Sounds corny, but the principal is the parent. He's also the president of the united or dis-united citizens of his nation-school, and he's responsible for the safety and wellbeing of all those under his jurisdiction. What can he do, but hope, pray and keep his fingers crossed?

In winter, when ice and snow fell, it covered the winding, twisting roads through the hills of Pendleton County. The superintendent, with my consultation, decided whether to have school, or call it off. We didn't want to take a chance, but often the decision was difficult and depended on the conditions of the roads. How much ice and snow is too much?

It snowed some one night leaving a few slick spots, but we decided to have school that day. Mrs. Morelle Hafer and her daughter, Jean Ann, who lived with her at the time, both taught at PHS. Jean Ann was ill that day and remained home, but Morelle began the cautious drive to school on that take-a-chance day. Not far from her home, a truck slid into her car. Our dedicated and beloved math teacher did not survive.

We should have called school off that day, but had to live with it from then on. In mid-morning, I made the announcement: Mrs. Morelle Hafer, our beloved teacher, was killed in a car accident this morning on the way to school. We have no choice but to carry on as best we can.

How could we carry on during such a day that seemed to never end? Sit there and teach and learn amidst the tears, the silence and the pain. The only consolation is that such extreme tragedies bring us closer together, and remind us how much we need other.

On November 22, 1963, I announced the death of President Kennedy. What could I say: We have no choice but to carry on as best we can. And our nation did as we reunited after that tremendous loss.

We had no choice other than carrying on each school day no matter what happened. The psychology in a school is rather fascinating. What determines a good or bad day? On perfectly clear sunshiny days, dark clouds do form. Who knows what the winds might blow in?

The days when we lost students and teachers were the

most difficult days, but we had other storms to weather, too—sometimes two or three per day.

It was a good day, the day before the Thanksgiving break. The happy students went outside to board their buses for home and a needed break. When I looked out the window, a boy attacked a girl with his fists, knocking her to the ground. It was a drug deal gone bad, and a good day gone much worse.

Young people are naturally excitable. They come screaming into a world where human nature too often remains in its infancy stage. There are also excitable teachers and principals who have not fully matured yet.

Human beings are social animals and interact with other humans and animals. The interactions can be civil and rewarding or conflicting and destructive. Schools are ripe for conflict simply due to the physical arrangements. When we cram mobs of young people in buildings and rooms, and keep them there for six hours trying to stuff knowledge into their heads, they will interact with those doing the stuffing. Where in society are there more human interactions per capita than in schools? And unlike most jobs and professions, a teacher can't take breaks and go hide somewhere. A principal can go to his office and lock the door, but his secretary might call him, as mine did one time: I just received a call saying that a man with a gun is on his way to school.

A doctor interacts with one patient at a time. A high school teacher interacts with up to thirty-five students for five periods each day—a total of 150 to 175 kids. Mrs. Norgood interacts with 153 human beings each day in her sophomore English classes. Most sophomore boys hate English and on her good days, she may have several dozen squabbles with them. If a principal is having a real bad day, he should lock himself in his office or go away to a workshop on conflict resolution.

Some teachers have severe personal problems. Perhaps you had one or more of these teachers. It's tough dealing with a long-time teacher who can't handle it anymore.

Eccentric Miss Funk, an ancient Latin teacher, who lost control of her classroom, preferred animals to her students. She kept about forty cats in her home, and the neighbors complained. To form better relationships with her students, she gave them all As at the last grading period, said she wanted them to feel good about themselves. The law then went to visit her cat house, and the story made the local paper.

After the superintendent and I discussed what to do with her, I called her in and said, Miss Funk, we have a problem.

She said, I know and I can't teach and take care of my house at the same time. Think I'll just resign and do something with those damn cats. Conflict resolved.

When a teacher and a student clash, the teacher can say, shape up or I'll send you to the principal. It was like that at my home. When my wonderful children acted up, my wonderful wife would tell them, Wait until your dad gets home.

I ran across this observation that made an impression: Whenever two or more persons of different rank are involved in a personal interchange, the one having superior rank determines the humanity of the relationship.

The principal outranks the teachers who outrank the students. We set the tone for the school. We have the power to determine the extent of a humane environment. There's a difference between authority and power. I was the principal and had the authority to tell students and teachers what to do. What if they didn't want to do what I said? Then I needed to create an environment and atmosphere that was conducive to not only learning, but liking and enjoying the naturally restrictive nature of a school. In classes where students give teachers fits, teachers have the power to better humanize that classroom. The most successful teachers are those who have the skills, temperament, and depth of character to humanize their learning environments. Not as simple as it sounds, but that approach often works wonders, and improves the teacher-student relationship, resulting in improved learning.

In contrast to a rigidly structured organization, what would happen if a school loosened up and became more exciting and fun?

I became a principal back when principals were trained to use an "iron fist." In the turbulent 1960s— when questioning authority became more common—that approach didn't work very well. What concerned me was not the type of fist applied—iron or a rubber glove—but that teaching and learning be interesting, even exciting. The teachers I remember who taught and inspired me more were demanding in a congenial way, especially if I thought they cared for me more than the subject they taught. There's not much a principal can do with a teacher who thinks: I wasn't hired to babysit, my job is to teach the subject I love and they'll learn it or else. It's their tough luck if they don't.

Obviously, a school must be well organized and orderly. Loosen up too much and things might go to pieces. But how tight should the structure be? An uptight principal tightens teachers who then tighten the screws on their students. When the tension reaches a critical point, something's got to give.

Education, as it was and essentially is, separates the sheep from the goats and the goats survive by nibbling the leftovers. Can a school be orderly in a more relaxed and inviting atmosphere? Do we continue force-feeding students information in textbooks, or will students take more responsibility for their own learning? Do I turn the whole shebang upside down or make excuses?

what Does a Hippie know?

Schools don't keep up with the times. We keep doing the same old things the same old way. About the only difference between a one-room school and a modern campus complex is the cafeteria and swimming pool. My mother walked two miles to school and I rode a bus over a bumpy gravel road. When I try explaining to my grandkids how tough it was back then, they leave the room and go online. The line I tried staying on was straight and narrow, but one with too many detour signs.

As society changes, schools lag way behind. Businesses and professions keep up with the times, or go out of business. Schools follow and perpetuate traditions, but stay in business. The first school began with a room, a teacher, and some students. When a school added rooms and teachers, it was necessary to hire a principal to coordinate everything and to keep order, using a big paddle if necessary. The teacher talked endlessly and students sat quietly listening to some of it. Parents didn't interfere, because teachers had absolute authority in their classroom unless the principal overruled them. If a little problem came up, the principal solved it on the spot. I went to that kind of school, but ten years later, when I became a principal, some things began to change.

When the Vietnam War broke out in the 1960s, people, particularly the young, asked why and began questioning authority, including the government and its military-industrial complex. This rebellion appeared early on university campuses, where students began to organize protests and sit-ins. Several university administration buildings were stormed and occupied. What better place for a longhaired hippie with beads dangling to light a weed than in a university president's chair? Make love, not war was the battle cry. Washington could not comprehend it. It didn't take long for the hippie philosophy to filter down into high schools. They didn't storm my office, but began to ask previously out-of-bound questions, and make statements such as: That's stupid. Some of it was and so I began to slowly change with the fast-changing times. Why did we keep doing things that made little sense, and how can we argue with make love, not war? Schools weren't war zones back then, but they were places where the academically strong survived, and the weak fell by the wayside.

Originally, the primary purpose of schooling involved

the development of the mind. Drill the basics, which might include a little Latin. There were plenty of labor jobs for those who couldn't make it. Then in the 1960s, segments of the public not only began to question authority, but also raised other pertinent questions regarding our institutions, including education. Why doesn't everyone have the right to an education? It's because schools were not equipped to educate all. What would we do with the handicapped and slow students in an academic setting? The accepted thinking was, They can't learn much of anything and certainly can't succeed. Well, here they came, whether we were ready or not.

The principal's task is to create an environment and atmosphere conducive to educating and molding the body, mind, heart, and soul of each child or youth. Then the focus changed to teaching the whole child and meeting each individual's needs.

The parents seemed to think, They're yours, don't let them drop out and walk the streets. And it would be nice if you could present a certificate of some sort to them after they've worn you down for twelve to fourteen years.

So, we had all of them and the whole of them to educate or contain until they were turned loose on society. That's asking a bit much when we might have a potential Ivy Leaguer sitting in the same class with Johnny who can't read.

Give our nation credit. In contrast to most other countries, America gathers all its children, transports them to schools, and expects the principals and teachers to educate every last one of them. In most other countries, students are tracked early on to an academic or vocational career. We take them all, which, supposedly, provides a better chance to realize the American dream.

Being all things to all children complicated everything. Students enter school unequal, but with equal opportunity? We were to simply take the whole child and meet their individual needs, thus ensuring equal opportunity. All whole children are different, and how do we know what their real needs are? We lumped them together and did the best we could.

To illustrate, Ms. England has thirty-three students in her fifth-period junior English class, and she loves the two girls sitting in the front row who write poetry. She ignores the two punks sprawling in the back, if they remain quiet. One of her girls is too scared to undergo a pregnancy test, and one is being sexually abused by her stepfather. Two boys appear to be high on something and half the class got little sleep last night. Some of her boys stay high, not on Emily Dickinson, but on the all-powerful hormonal interaction with Emily across the aisle dressed in a skirt way too short. One of her students is struggling with his sexual orientation. Five of her students live in foster homes, or with aunts, uncles, Gramps, or friends. Eight live in one-parent homes, which might include mom's boyfriend or dad's girlfriend. Some of the homes are unfit for the pets roaming around. Twelve of her students live in good homes and are "normal." Multiply that class by five, and she sees 165 students with diverse needs, which she should meet. This student may need a stable home more than anything, but that's not her problem.

Open your book to page fourteen, Ms. England says. Oh, you lost your book again, Ricky?

When a student says he lost his book, do not ask him to explain how, when, where, or why. It will take valuable instructional time. Tell him to take out a sheet of paper and a pencil, and take notes.

You don't carry paper? Okay, go to the office, Ricky, and explain to Mr. C that you are ill equipped to perform in my classroom.

Does Mr. C say, I'm ill-equipped to deal with you, Ricky, but the next time you go to class without a piece of paper, I'll kill you? No, he loans Ricky a sheet of paper and says, Get out of here, out of my life. What does Mr. C do to or for the Rickys in his school? Please tell me.

Technology began to make a big change in schools in the 1960s. In 1962 at PHS, we had only one microscope in the science department. And what a difference a new copy machine made in the office. Before, we hand-copied student transcripts to send to colleges. Showing a rented film in class was a rare treat for students. Thirty years later, I asked a grandson after his first day in kindergarten if they had computers in his room. He said they did, but they weren't on the Internet yet. Today, a student can't succeed without a smartphone. Back then, we learned from books.

Classroom dynamics changed from the traditional lecture-recite-memorize method. No one really knows what goes on in a classroom unless he or she is sitting in one. Through the years, I observed thousands of classes, not only to evaluate teachers, but also to help teachers improve their teaching techniques. Sitting in was usually enlightening, fun, and often funny. Most—most I said—teachers are human, conscientious, and competent, and they teach in their own unique way. It helps if teachers like kids and get a kick out of them, but some don't. When teaching becomes a chore and a drag, they should move on and do something that doesn't requires people in their hair.

Her students called her Crazy Emily. She thought Emily Dickinson's poetry could improve humanity if her students could learn and comprehend what was in some of her 1,775 poems.

Class, go with me to poem number 370 as Emily writes about capacity, beautifully:

Heaven is so far of the Mind—
That were the Mind dissolved—
The Site—of it—by Architect
Could not again be proved—
Tis vast—as our Capacity . . .

Now class, this is a perfect opportunity to see the relationship between heaven and a mind dissolved. And Ricky, don't you understand your vastness for capacity?

Yes, but I don't understand how a mind can dissolve.

I'll tell you how . . .

But another hand goes up from the back as the bell rings. When bells ring for prizefighters and teachers, it prevents knockouts.

Students also interact with teachers outside their classrooms. Mrs. Bertha Barton, who taught English before high school boys began carrying condoms in their billfolds, sent Cindy to my office with a note that read: When I entered my classroom this morning, I found the enclosed condom hanging on my doorknob. It's a sick world. Thanks, Bertha

Yes, it is a sick world, Mrs. Barton, but we must continue trying to change it.

The world has changed. Could I work in today's schools? Only if humans taught; robots can't replace the Crazy Emilys of the world.

CHAPTER 9

Turning School Inside Out

The social and institutional turbulence and disorder intensified during the 1960s, led by the young who demanded that the social and governmental order be dramatically changed. This movement had a domino effect and it trickled down into high schools. I was young, too, and had let my hair grow out a bit longer than my previous military burr and flattop cuts. I agreed that the high school establishment was stale, outdated, and archaic, so I thought, why not change it inside out or upside down? Maybe I was a radical.

Some people develop a philosophy of life. The great essayist, Montaigne, wrote that his philosophy was to live well and die well. The institutionally established high schools seemed to not be living very well; they were sterile places with staff who were going through the motions. Since education has been considered a salvation of civilizations, critics began writing about what was wrong with schools. I read this stuff and agreed with most of it.

Beatle Paul McCartney said that never once did anyone make it clear what he was being educated for. Robert Frost said that a good teacher knows how to get more out of a student by surrounding him with an atmosphere of expectation than by putting the screws on him. Christopher Jencks said that the primary basis for evaluating a school should be whether students and teachers find it a pleasant place to be.

Another critic saw the teacher-student relationship as a form of institutionalized dominance and subordination. Another criticism: Failure is structured into the American system of public education. Losers are essential to the success of winners. And another: The most important characteristic that nearly all schools share is a preoccupation with order and control. Education experts and critics wrote about the glazed look in classrooms, the assault on the personality, and the forms of violence—humiliation, insults, embarrassments, and judgments. Erik Erikson said that the most deadly of all possible sins is the mutilation of a child's spirit.

I tried being nonviolent with my students and teachers. I didn't want to mutilate their spirits. I wanted to lift their spirits. In order for students to like school, they must be successful, but we often put them in situations where they fail. It's the same old routine, the same old lock-step pattern.

It's tedious, monotonous, and boring for many students and teachers. It bothered me that a majority of our students would much rather be anywhere else than in school.

One student told me, I can't wait to quit school and go into destruction work. My brother quit and he makes $6.50 per hour laying blocks. He meant construction work; his schoolwork was what was destructive to him.

We had students who quit school and actually made more money at a local fertilizer plant than what our teachers made. I could not subscribe to the philosophy of make it tough on them, because life is tough.

What could I do to keep order and make PHS a pleasant place where students wanted to be? And how could we teach lessons that were enjoyable? We could try turning the locked-in structure upside down, and change teacher and student schedules, breaking away from the traditional one-hour time frame for each class to a flexible modular schedule. After about a year's study, our staff agreed to try this totally different approach. It was like taking our old humdrum lives and changing them to completely new and dynamic ones.

A few other high schools across the United States had also changed to various types of modular scheduling, breaking away from the traditional one-hour class periods. Modern education experts proposed variations of this new plan, and the University of Iowa established a newfangled computer program to schedule this totally different arrangement. I went there and came back with schedules for our teachers and students that looked somewhat similar to plans for a moon shot.

Flexible modular scheduling is quite complicated as it changes the typical six periods of one-hour duration into twenty periods or mods of twenty-minute duration. A traditional schedule is repeated every school day, the same old thing day after day. A modular schedule is structured on a six-day cycle—Days one, two, three, four, five, and six. Student and teacher schedules change each day of the cycle for six days and then the pattern is repeated for the next six days. Each morning, when giving the announcements, I began by saying, Remember, today is day two. Follow your day two schedule. Day two could be on a Monday, Tuesday, or any other day of the week.

Before continuing with an explanation of our totally new system, I will make a few comments about what most high schools—and particularly rural high schools—were all about. Our superintendent kept reminding me of the importance of three Bs—buses, beans (the cafeteria), and basketball. Most complaints and phone calls from parents were about those three things. Reading, writing, and arithmetic ranked down toward the bottom of the list. Weak teachers were tolerated unless one went completely off his rocker. But a mean school bus driver, inept cafeteria manager serving hog slop, or a losing basketball coach consumed most of the discussions at school board meetings.

It's difficult to explain how important basketball is in

Kentucky. In the hills and the little towns and villages, the high school basketball team was a prime source of community pride. Later when I became a principal in Indiana, basketball ranked higher than corn, soybeans, and religion. The whole state devoured Hoosier Hysteria and March Madness as the hungry consume food.

In both states, a "good school" had a winning basketball team. A losing coach was discussed at school board meetings as being detrimental to the educational progress. A losing English or math teacher kept his job. The point is that good schools, in the eyes of taxpayers, kept school buses running on time, served food the children might eat, and won a basketball tournament. Of course, parents wanted their children learning things from books, but the quality of teaching and learning seldom became an issue.

A good school principal believed in God, but he could not overtly preach. A good school with a good principal also fought crime, did not permit sex in any form including lewd library books, and prohibited alcoholic beverages within five miles of school grounds. High school students experimented with all of these sins. A basketball star caught drinking ripped the whole community apart. A pregnant cheerleader was quietly sent away. A good school also had a godly principal, who should be seen in church. Needing all the help I could get, I went each Sunday to ask God for deliverance.

A principal must stay on his toes to prevent students from finding ways to sneak alcohol onto school property.

Each year, the PHS seniors took a trip to Washington DC to learn to appreciate our forefathers and the Constitution, and look at monuments. During this trip, chaperones needed to be ever alert and prevent male and female students from intermingling in hotel rooms, and they also needed to detect any hint of Kentucky bourbon.

One year, on the day of departure, our seniors brought their suitcases to school, put them in a storage room, and when the last bell rang, they boarded buses for a trip to Cincinnati. They would then board a train to our nation's capital to see what Congress does. Chaperoning something like this was going beyond the call of duty, but dedicated teachers did it for the kids.

I was sitting in my office on the day of departure when the two class sponsors came in with a suitcase and closed the door. They shook the suitcase and you could hear what sounded like liquid gurgling. They opened it and took out seven pints of Old Crow, whereupon I blew sky high.

I'll get to the bottom of this, cancel the trip, and call the parents and the sheriff.

No, no, we've got it under control, the senior sponsor said. We've confiscated the whiskey, and the kids can't buy more anywhere near the White House.

I cooled down. They gave me the Old Crow; what could I do with it except pour it on the sacred school grounds?

We outsmarted them, didn't we? Or my two young sponsors did. Years later, I saw Steve again, the senior, who owned the bourbon-filled suitcase. He was one of the best senior boys in the class, and later became a college professor. We had a good laugh, and Steve, somewhat red-faced, explained that the rogue senior boys talked him into carrying their liquor. No one would ever suspect him or search his suitcase. We outsmarted them, and that is a valuable lesson. We had to outsmart the young and immature to have any chance at all of surviving. We had to stay one step ahead of them, but sometimes they could outrun us.

Why do schools think they are obligated to take teenagers on overnight trips, put them in hotel rooms, lock the doors, and stand guard all night? It's all a part of the total learning process, but why Washington? Who knows, there could be another Lincoln or Nixon in the senior class.

In the summer of 1968, I was selected by the National Association of Secondary School Principals to help sponsor 133 high school juniors and student council members from throughout the United States on an eight-week European Tour for World Understanding. At that time, there must have been a better way to promote world understanding, but the twenty-eight sponsor-chaperones, composed of teachers, counselors, principals, and nurses, sacrificed themselves to try to bring peace to the world. It was not peaceful or understandable, but it was wonderful, and America's Student Council representatives were great, once we wore them down. I learned that in most respects, the young in all parts of the world have similar characteristics, goals, and desires, despite cultural and language differences.

Young people get along; most adults don't. It was my first trip abroad. After retiring from trying to understand the world of education, I took fifteen more trips abroad, and realize that as my final trip approaches, I won't need a passport. My record is on file up there.

Want some more stories about immaturity? Theirs and mine? I've got a bunch, but this book is about education, preparation for life. Something about the life of the young, though, turned me on. I think it was the potential of every student in the school, the potential to be a good person and have a good life. Rank in class does not weed out the good from the bad. The lowest-ranked student has potential.

I can't do anything, he thinks.

You have more potential than you think you do. Maybe you can't make the honor roll, but you can be successful and the best person in the class.

I saw many low-ranked students rise to the top in the human-being category. It's like the girl who said, This crazy teacher thought I was smarter than I was, so I was. Building confidence get results.

The flexible modular schedule brought about a new way of life to our school. One theory of this type of re-organizing classes, students, and teachers is that students will have the opportunity to take greater responsibility for their own learning. The locked-step, force-feeding of information into their minds changed to leading and inspiring students to take more responsibility for their own learning.

Students met in large groups, small groups, and lab groups, and had independent study or unscheduled time, which averaged about 30 percent of their school day. Parents asked, Won't students goof off, waste time, and commit crimes during this unscheduled or free time when you don't even know where they are? It was free time, and it did take some time, but we did a lot of preparation and instruction in preparing our students to take more responsibility for their own progress. We said, Use your time wisely and it will pay off for you. Some didn't, but most did. Some did nothing, but that got old and boring. Eventually, the goof-offs began to use their time to their advantage.

When we converted to the modular schedule in the middle of the year, I was so proud of our school. It was like being born again. We became a national Title III demonstration school and had visitors from many other schools. They were amazed at how our students handled their unscheduled time. It was an orderly place and a more pleasant place than what it had been.

The visitors were also amazed that the student lockers did not have locks on them. A handful of students had locks on their lockers, but they weren't really needed, because our people were good people, who trusted others. Of all the good things about our school, students and teachers didn't see the need to lock themselves in. It was an atmosphere where students and teachers wanted to be, a place where we felt free to teach and learn.

In the fall of 1970, four teachers from Jeffersonville

High School in Indiana visited PHS. When they were ready to leave, one said, I don't know what we're going to do. We're building a fabulous new school and going to modular scheduling, but our principal resigned.

Why I called the superintendent's office there, I'll never know, but two months later, I walked into the old, decrepit Jeffersonville High School building as their new principal.

where's the Principal's office?

Moving from the country to a city can be an adjustment. You can take a country boy out of the country, but you can't take the country out of him, said a city person. But if you take a country boy out of the country, he may not be certain where he is. After ten good years at PHS, it was like going from an environment with a few brush fires to an incinerator that could melt steel. When things got a little tough at the country school, I took a walk in the woods to get my head back on straight. But at Jeffersonville, if I walked down the middle of a busy city street, I ran the risk of being run over.

The social and political turbulence of the 1960s carried over into the '70s with protests, unrest, rebellion, and racial strife. After Watergate, the new unelected president, Gerald Ford said, I must say the state of our Union is not good, and I must say that the state of our schools is not what it should be.

Why did I decide to undertake such a monumental challenge? Why did Lincoln think he could save the Union? Although I was imported from the South, it was not a Civil War. The good people in the Jeffersonville, Indiana, community welcomed and supported me. Jeffersonville is directly across the Ohio River from Louisville and part of a sprawling urban community. There was nothing I could do but dive in and swim for dear life, but where to begin? I could try learning the names of the 2,700 students. But first, I needed to learn the names of the 155 staff members. It took months.

Who are you, I asked?

I'm one of your assistant principals, he said.

You are? Tell me about this place. He did and it was not a pretty sight. There had been protests, lawsuits over long hair, and general unrest, including minor racial strife. About 10 percent of the JHS student population was black. Only five black students attended PHS. The JHS buildings had fallen apart and it was a dreary place during that cold winter of 1970–71.

When Dr. Foust, the superintendent, interviewed me, he took me to the old JHS where students milled around outside. The school was so crowded it didn't have enough rooms or desks for all the students, and when not in class, they wandered around town. The JHS campus included seven different makeshift buildings scattered about, including the town's old Taylor High School, an all-black school before integration. It had fireplaces (unused) in each room. The old gym, known as the field house, seated 5,000 spectators, and the Red Devils had a good basketball team with a loyal following—one source of pride. The community, however, had great expectations for the fabulous new school and the future looked bright—if I could shine some light.

When the superintendent stopped outside the old school, he asked, Do you want to go in?

I said, no, knowing that if I went in the old main building, I probably wouldn't accept the job if it was offered. He then took me to the new school under construction. It had ten acres of floor space and would be one of the most modern schools in Indiana. It had everything, and was like moving from an army barracks to the Pentagon.

On December 1, 1970, my first day as principal at JHS, I parked my car near the old school, walked in, and asked a student roaming around, where's the principal's office? Down there, he said. When I walked into the outer office, the secretary, who recognized me from my photos in the newspapers, practically fainted. When she led me, like leading the blind, to my office, I sat down and thought, what do I do now? I'm the principal and only know two people here by name.

It was very difficult to leave my rural home where I grew up and worked with people I knew. Uprooting my family and moving to a city and new schools for my wife and four young children was exciting in a way, but also traumatic. Was I up to the challenge? Too late now; we had packed up and moved from an idyllic life to the unknown. It was like going from a place warmed by sunshine to a place temporarily clouded over. No sunshine yet, but I found rays of hope.

I did have and do have a personal life in addition to a life deep in the heart of a schoolhouse. I had a family and a home where I slept and I also had a dog. Here's a dog story that might help explain some of my limited human traits, particularly as they relate to animals. Our dog was a black border collie, named Black Dog.

We had lived about a mile from PHS. When I'd go home after school, Black Dog would hear my car coming and he'd run and be the first to greet me, pawing at the door before I could open it. It made him so happy to be near me, happier than my teachers, students, and family were. Dogs can think. Black dog said, Think I'll go to school with him tomorrow to be closer to him. Living in the country, he roamed free, and he decided to run to school each early morning and wait for me under my car. But that was not close enough. He then began running to school and lying down at the main entrance to the school outside my office window.

When students arrived, they'd say, Good morning, Black Dog. He became another school mascot in addition to the fierce Wildcats.

Moving broke our hearts. I explained to the children that Black Dog had been free to roam the countryside. When we moved to the city, he'd be locked in a doghouse like a hardened criminal. He'd be tied in a little solitary cell in the backyard, living on stale bread and water. Why don't we see if Uncle Tommy will keep him here where he can be free after we move? Tommy, my brother-in-law, who farmed the family farm where I grew up, agreed to keep Black Dog.

He chained Black Dog in a barn stall (dogs gnaw ropes) until he bonded with his new master. A phone call: Black Dog had somehow broken the chain, dug a tunnel under the barn to escape, and was now free again. What won't creatures do to be free?

Ten days later, another phone call: They found Black Dog lying outside the PHS door. He had traveled ten miles to find me. I traveled a hundred miles to bring him back to me. End of story, but there is a moral. If you ever feel unappreciated, misunderstood, and unloved, God's creatures can help you. And if you do stupid things, your dog will forgive you.

My task as principal at JHS the remainder of that year was to prepare the teachers and students to move into the new school the next year with a flexible modular scheduling system. It was something like planning the D-day invasion. Oh, I also had to discipline bad students, weed out bad teachers, and go to basketball games wearing a red tie. The community questioned why Indiana searched Kentucky to find a principal when Kentucky had a reputation for backwardness. But I tried using all the intelligence I had to gain their trust and hoped they thought I knew what I was doing.

Before I went to JHS, the decision had been made to convert to modular scheduling, and the new building was designed to accommodate it with four rooms that seated over a hundred students for large-group instruction.

Briefly, this is how modular scheduling works. As mentioned earlier, students and teachers meet in large groups, small groups, and lab groups, and they had unscheduled time. Lab groups and shop classes usually met for four mods (eighty minutes), which gave sufficient time to work with equipment, conduct experiments, and dissect animals. A large group might meet for three mods (sixty minutes) to present new material, show films, or have guest speakers. (Teachers could show a film the traditional way and do it five times, while they sat and dozed.) Doctors, nurses, and police spoke to large-group health classes, and two members of Congress spoke to senior government classes in large groups of about two hundred.

Research reveals that attention spans last less than the typical thirty-minute TV sitcom episode. Small groups of twelve to fifteen usually met for two mods (thirty-five or forty minutes with five minutes for passing time) to discuss, ask questions, interact, and exchange ideas. Small groups were often arranged in a circle without the teacher standing over them, saying open your book to page ten, and Jason, you read it to the class. It's page ten. Jason, please wake up.

Group dynamics were stressed where students could talk openly, rather than listening to teachers all day.

Don't sit down and shut up, but tell me what you think, express your thoughts and explain what Emily Dickinson meant by The Heart is Capital of the Mind.

Teachers and students became more like human beings again, and were less bored by going through the motions.

Both teachers and students had 25 to 35 percent of their time unscheduled. With less time in classes, it was important to make the most of that time, with no time to kill as was the norm. It wasn't free time as such, but independent study for students. Students had to learn to take more responsibility for their own learning. Obviously, this took some time, but most students began using their time on schoolwork. At morning announcements, I usually closed with, Remember to use your time wisely. It's to your advantage.

At a mod break every twenty minutes—signaled by a tone sound over the intercom, not a loud bell—about one-third of the students moved to another room for another class, or if unscheduled, to an open room. During a traditional six-period day, all 2,700 students moved six times: pushing, shoving, and grabbing in a sea of humanity.

Where did an unscheduled student go during his free time? It was not free time: It was independent study. The critics said, That's a joke. High school students will create more problems when turned loose. They'll smoke more dope; we'll have more teenage mothers; juvenile delinquency rates will go sky high. If a seventeen-year-old can join the army and fight wars, he should be able to learn how to be more responsible for his own learning, shouldn't he?

During independent study time, each student chose where he or she would go. They could go to the library, a study hall, or to a favorite teacher's room, and sit in on another class. They could go to a typing room and practice typing, to a shop and work on a project, or to a music or art room or the gym, and help a favorite teacher. They could even help tutor other students, which some did.

About nineteen open rooms were available to students each mod. In addition to the spacious library, the dial-access-retrieval room, two quiet study halls, one buzz study hall in the cafeteria for upper classmen, and two resource centers, were open. The one commandment: You must be in a room.

Students also had a schedule of open rooms. It was rather amazing how teachers and students came together in our open school. It had a humanizing aspect. The traditional approach where teachers talked, lectured and said, Do as I say, began to break down into a much more relaxed atmosphere, as teachers had more time and opportunity to personally interact with students. Students also had more time and opportunity to realize teachers were human beings. The principal worked on his human skills during his free time.

The library stayed full. What a surprise compared to the old way. The spacious library had a room for a modern dial-access-retrieval system. Teachers often taped their lectures and presentations, and students could dial up, listen and review, or check out the tapes if they had been absent.

The modular system gave teachers and teaching teams greater opportunity to be more creative, breaking from the stifling go-by-the-book tradition. They made some exciting things happen and students responded favorably, or most did.

Remember, you are not told where to go, but you have the freedom to go where you want to go as long as it's a room in this building. It's your education and we're here to help you.

Like ants or busy bees, they began to go where they felt more at home. A school that is a kind of home away from home is likely to get better results.

Teachers developed and wrote LAPs, learning activity packets. Okay, it was a fancy name for homework, but an LAP was designed to direct a student's independent study. Teachers worked together as teams, taking advantage of strengths and maybe hiding a few weaknesses.

For example, one of our US history teams created all sorts of motivational presentations for large groups of 150 students or more. At the theater, they depicted the assassination of Abraham Lincoln. Tall and lanky, I played Lincoln. It was quite dramatic when John Wilkes Booth shot me. Years later, I'd see former graduates on the street. They'd frequently greet me with Hi, Abe. During another large-group motivational presentation in a home economics class, the USDA actually flew a representative from Washington to give the presentation. Educating the young is not a waste of tax dollars.

We had many visitors to our busy beehive, and no one got stung. Initially, rumors were that the new JHS was chaos in motion, kids gone wild.

Come and see for yourself, I said.

When they did, I heard, It's not what I thought it would be. Kids are not running all over the place. They're busy and happy and teachers are, too.

However, those first few months were rough. It was a monumental adjustment, and some students didn't do well. Things did begin smoothing out after the initial shock of the new system wore off, and students learned how to take more responsibility for their own learning. And it didn't hurt that the Red Devil basketball team began winning tournaments. A community doesn't often rally around a superior English department or a dynamic new math teacher, but winning basketball games in Indiana is like winning the battle at Gettysburg.

The Red Devils kept winning tournaments and went to the final game at Indiana University's Assembly Hall where Bobby Knight reigned as a God-like figure. We lost the state championship by three points, and, in addition to that, during the game, God sent a freak snow and ice storm over Bloomington. The police contacted me and said, Don't take those three hundred kids home in school buses; it's too dangerous. The IU athletic director told me we could stay in Assembly Hall. The girls slept on mats in the wrestling room and the boys in the bleachers. I asked Tom, my assistant, to go buy six hundred donuts and three hundred cartons of milk and he did. What a long night it was, but the students and chaperones were great, as most all young people and teachers are. That's why I didn't sell insurance or work for the government.

After the first trying year at the new JHS, we established an alternative school in one of the buildings at the old JHS downtown for those students who couldn't or wouldn't adjust to the modular program. About a hundred students enrolled in the alternative program and four teachers volunteered to teach them. At graduation that year, twenty-nine seniors from the alternative school received diplomas. I was as proud of them as I was of the honor students. When he'll-never-make-it makes it, you feel a sense that maybe all those times you said—You can do it—paid off.

Innovation was the name of our game. For those who believed we should put God back in our schools, we offered a course in the Bible as literature, and thirty students enrolled. And who says young people aren't interested in the environment? We offered a course in environmental science, and nearly three hundred students signed up, and a course in advanced health for students interested in a medical-related career.

We had over thirty teaching teams composed of two to

four team members. Each team had a mod or two scheduled to plan during each six-day cycle. Specific strengths of each team member were utilized. For example, one health teacher was particularly skilled in presenting new material to large groups, while other team members assumed other responsibilities.

For students with special needs, we formed interdisciplinary teams to teach in block programs. For example, a math, history, and English teacher met with groups of sophomores for an eight-mod block of time in an English, history, and math core program.

Teachers liked team teaching or most did. They enjoyed working together as a team and learning from each other. Students liked it, too. If you had a boring teacher for an hour every day in the traditional system, it was seldom that you were taught by a team with three boring teachers in the new system.

At both PHS and JHS, we conducted evaluations to determine the effect of the modular system. We were particularly concerned with standardized achievement test scores, whether they went up or down. The evaluations revealed that the scores remained about the same, but attitudes changed for the better.

We had no statistical evidence to determine whether there had been an increase or decrease in academic achievement; however, we saw evidence that teachers and students preferred the modular system over the traditional one. At JHS, 82 percent of the faculty preferred the modular system with modifications, by incorporating a more traditional block-type system for about 20 percent of the students who needed more structure and direction. A survey of the entire student body revealed that 94 percent preferred the modular system, and 82 percent indicated they learned more. Skeptics would say students just like the unscheduled time so they can goof off. We told skeptics to visit a traditional locked-down school and observe the environment. Then, before making judgment, visit our school and compare our learning atmosphere.

CHAPTER 11

Only Five Rules to Follow

A good school is an orderly school. It took time, but, after we made the adjustment and worked out a few kinks, our students were orderly for the most part, and I was proud of them. We had only five rules to follow and one was: Be happy. Schools should be happy places, because if they are not, it's an ongoing battle.

Schools can become uptight places, filled with tension, and many are. Humans of all ages have a tendency to get excited and throw occasional fits. I think younger people are easier to deal with when you sit down and talk with them. They seem to have more sense than does Congress, school board members, taxpayers and parents whose children do no wrong. Too many older people already know everything. Teachers having continuous conflicts with students don't have or use much common sense.

How many times have I heard struggling teachers say,

He doesn't respect me? Could it be because you don't respect him? A misbehaving student knows he's misbehaving. Call him in.

You're misbehaving, aren't you?

I guess so.

It's easy to correct, isn't it?

I guess so.

I don't want to call your parents. Will you behave?

I guess so.

You guess?

Okay, I will.

Problem usually solved.

Most schools publish a thick student handbook to prevent lawyers from getting involved. These handbooks list crimes and punishments, but students don't usually read rule books. It's a waste of paper. The preppies will do stupid things and act up, too. One thing they do not want you to do is say to them, Before you can come back to school, you must bring a parent with you.

Near his graduation, the senior class president wore a bathrobe to school. What he wore underneath, I do not know. I phoned his father, a respected physician.

We have a concern with your son. Can you come?

When he arrived, I sent for his bathrobe-clad son. The usual excuse, I didn't have time to get dressed and didn't want to be late for school. The physician-father looked as if he might explode, but the class president lived to graduate.

Meek little Robert wore a T-shirt to school with F__k you printed in small letters all over it. Called his mother and called Robert in.

Yes, I know, I bought the shirt for him. He's so shy, and we thought it might help him become more assertive.

She had a good point, but I told her that we had to keep bad sex words out of our school. What would you tell her, f__k you? Robert became assertive enough to make it to a university and major in philosophy. Principals *have* to be assertive and philosophers should be.

Most parents support the school. In the old days, if you got a whipping at school, you'd get another one when you went home. People believed that the teacher and principal could do no wrong. Yes, they could and do. Things began to change in the 1960s. A few parents of brilliant and perfect children who could do no wrong began questioning everything the school did.

I'll sue you . . .

Some did. A few cases reached the Supreme Court, including the students' right to freedom of speech and what could be published in the school newspaper.

In one school's newspaper the principal, a friend of mine, saw a photo of a jackass superimposed with his head on the front page. This was cause for a new school rule: students shall not portray the principal as a jackass or anything else that would demean the character and integrity of the school and its leader. Schools are like the larger society; laws are made to be broken and most are.

Why fight it? So, at Jeffersonville High School, I reduced the rules to five simple ones:

1. Behave.
2. Don't worry.
3. Be happy.
4. Do your work.
5. Respect everyone.

These rules just about cover it all. There's nothing happier than a happy school. Since the principal is the leader, he should appear to be happy whether he is or is not. I did my best and remained happy except when students and teachers violated any of my five rules. The following are some rule-violation episodes I remember:

Rule 5—Respect everyone—is a tough one, but respecting everyone prevents all kinds of problems. When Amy called Jamie a bitch, Jamie slapped Amy. Don't ever call a girl a bitch or slut.

You two violated rule five, didn't you?

I gave this oft-repeated life sermon many times: Life is too short to be in conflict with others. If you like making enemies, then I pity you. I like to make friends and need all I can get. What if I called you a name or hit you? Both of you are bright, attractive, and fine young ladies, and I respect you. What if I didn't? You wouldn't want that, would you? Here's what I want both of you to do. After you leave this room, I want you to respect each other. It's really simple;

you just go about your business and, although you may not like each other, you will respect each other, won't you?

Yes.

Yes.

It usually worked.

Bullies don't respect anyone. It can begin in the early years and become a serious problem, particularly in the early teen years. Students who are bullied hesitate to tell anyone. A minister and his wife came in, nervous, anxious, and deeply concerned.

Who was the bully, I asked?

They hesitated, but revealed a name.

I'll take care of it.

I called the two girls in and closed the door, while the parents sat outside fidgeting.

The girls heard my get-along-in-life speech, and when I opened the door, the bully and the preacher's daughter together approached the tense parents.

Mom, it's all settled now.

What do you mean, it's settled?

The bully said, Yes, it's settled.

The two girls smiled.

The minister seemed to hesitate in believing it was another one of God's miracles. But God should provide more time inside a school to explain why and how to respect and love thy neighbors.

Rule 2—Don't worry—is another tough one. You can see it in their faces and their anxious behaviors.

I thought I had a few worries, but some of the stories I've heard from worried teens, teachers, and parents put my worries in a much different perspective. A father brought in his daughter Jennifer and said nothing as he threw a Marlboro box packed with joints on my desk.

She brought this home, so what are you going to do with her?

I'm not going to do anything with her. What are you going to do with her?

Okay, I'll help you.

But what is a school miracle worker do when parents reach their wits' end? Stay calm and use our wits to help solve family, school, social, national, and world problems. It takes time, patience, wits, and luck.

This father was lucky; Jennifer made it.

Mr. Kilgore taught history and began having emotional and mental problems that finally forced him over the edge. The teacher across the hall came to my office and said that I needed to go talk to Mr. Kilgore. We had noticed that he'd become rather nervous and anxious—not the same man. When I went to his room, he was over the edge, confused and irrational.

I finally convinced him to go with me so we could talk. I called his wife on a phone outside my office. She was alarmed, but aware of his condition and did not know what to do other than hope it would pass. After a couple of hours, we finally convinced him to go with us to a psychiatric hospital two hours away. I arrived home that day after midnight, totally drained. It was one of my toughest school days ever. Fortunately, he recovered and returned to work.

A principal doesn't worry, because he doesn't have time after listening all day to the worries of those outside his office.

Yes, you can come in and talk to me in this worry-free zone.

Worried students need someone to talk to. It's not that simple, but it is.

Teens worry about everything—weight, looks, being liked by the people they like.

Amy, you look worried. Tell me why.

I can't do it.

Do what?

Give a report in front of the class.

Yes, you can, I know you can. Here's what I want you to do. Tomorrow, come back and give the report to me.

I can't.

Yes, you can, I know you can.

Amy came back the next day, stood shaking in front of my desk, and forced her report out of her mouth.

You did good and that wasn't so bad, was it? Now quit worrying so much; it's against the rules. Come back in after your talk and tell me how it went.

She came back, smiling and with a gleam in her eye. It went okay.

Remember when you were young? What didn't you worry about? Many students have serious things to worry about and see no way out. And many of these young people go unnoticed.

Ernie, a senior, was using a pay phone in the hallway during class, and it seemed something was wrong. When I tapped him on the shoulder, he turned and looked at me. The disconsolate expression on his face revealed his pain.

Come to the office with me and we'll talk.

Finally, he said he had to talk to someone and had been trying to call a friend.

I feel so bad and have been thinking about suicide, he said.

You're in a class thinking of suicide, and the teacher says, get to work.

I called his mother, and eventually Ernie got back on track.

Larry, a senior, asked to see me. He was quiet, somewhat shy, and seemed to have few friends. He sat there, just staring at me. What did he want? I waited a bit and then asked how everything was going.

Silently staring into space, he mumbled some trivial thing. Strange. He obviously had something he wanted to tell me, but what gnawed at him couldn't come out.

A few days later, I learned that his adoptive father had been cited for sexually abusing Larry and his brother since they were very young, and all those years he lived with it, not knowing what to do. How many kids in our school, all schools, live with sexual abuse, but are too terrified to tell?

You can lead a horse to water, but you can't make him

drink. If you lead students to an education in a school, some will drink it in when they're there. Seniors get anxious at graduation time, and don't use their mature, high-school educated heads. A group of leading seniors needed to practice for senior class night.

Sure, you can practice on the theater stage.

Can we serve donuts and punch?

Sure you can.

As they were practicing, a moral senior came to my office and said, Mr. C, you need go to the theater.

I did, and then called two wonderful parents of two lovely senior girls.

Mrs. Mother, will you come and pick up your outstanding senior daughter? She's drunk.

Why should we think an irresponsible senior would pour a fifth of vodka in the punch bowl before school even starts?

Any high-school principal will tell you that when the last senior in cap and gown with diploma in hand marches out of the gym door, he feels like Jonah felt when the whale burped.

If a student is unhappy, worried, disrespectful, and misbehaving, he has a problem, and the school does, too. What do you do to or with him? Some students obeyed all the rules except the fourth rule: do your work.

Frequently, parents and teachers say, He quit working and won't do anything. I don't know what's wrong with him. Seniors frequently want school to be over before it's over. They quit schoolwork, but hold successful jobs in the community, working in fast food places or bagging groceries, smart enough to separate perishables from cans. I had one senior boy who was a night manager at a convenience store, but he would not learn about the Bill of Rights.

We had two days to go and Clarence was one credit short. He ran to Mr. Marshall, and asked if there was anything he could do to pass government and graduate.

Yes, there is. Read this book and report back to me.

Clarence had never read a book in his life, but three hours later, he reported back to Mr. Marshall: I read it.

He did learn what government does in summer school and he's now contributing to society.

One year at JHS, the local NAACP asked to meet with me. Letters had been sent to the parents of students at risk for not meeting graduation requirements, including the parents of five black seniors. It was an injustice, unfair and a racial thing, said the NAACP. Actually, the five students had quit doing their schoolwork.

Yes, I know, I said. We've encouraged them, counseled them, warned them, but for whatever reason, they refuse to complete their work. The NAACP understood it was not a racial thing when I told them we had twenty-one white seniors in the same boat.

You do?

In every high school, most students do well, cause few problems, graduate and get decent jobs, marry and have kids who graduate from high school. In every high school, maybe 10 percent of students are like Vernon.

How many times did I explain it this way?

Vernon, take a book to class, any book, sit there and shut up, write words on a paper, any words, and turn it in with your name on it. You'll get a D-, a diploma, and then you can go out into the world driving a car to a decent job, raising a family with kids. You are a senior with one month to go. Vernon, this time next year, you might bring a child into the world. Get serious about your life. Would you want Vernon Jr. goofing off when he goes to school?

If a student obeyed the five rules for four years, at least in part, I announced their name at graduation. They walked across the platform, tassels swaying, and families shouting and cheering like unruly fans at an Indiana or Kentucky basketball game.

The world little knows what we do or say here in the name of education. Graduation for many indicates twelve years of endurance, barely making it. Academic success had little or nothing to do with it. Vernon still won't read, but he could if he wanted to. Teachers and principals who endure squeeze more of them through the confines of a school out into the real and changing world. Somehow, most eventually find themselves, find their place.

Every society and school has its factions, social groups, cliques. The jocks rule some schools and consider music, art, and drama students sissies. The hippie-druggy cultures reinforce each other and segregate in the darkest corners.

Near-the-bottom students resent brainy types, whose friends have high SAT scores. The hoods hang out and hang on until you hang them out to dry. Black students eat together in the cafeteria, and shop students will not eat with the college bound. In-love students are late to every class. In such a social milieu, the principal must promote harmony and equality.

It costs more to imprison a person than to educate him. Prisons are for those who break the laws. The streets are for those students who fight, steal, extort, destroy property, possess weapons, and possess or use drugs and alcohol on school property.

Until the 1990s, many schools had a smoking area before school and at lunchtime for students who had parental approval. It helped settle students' nerves, and it was better than having the thick blue haze in restrooms. Smoking on school grounds is prohibited now, but some students continue to light up, risking expulsion and possibly graduation.

Why did you take that chance?

I don't know.

Expulsion is no big deal to those who've been beat around. Don't have to worry with school and teachers anymore. Dealing with the perpetual and severest problem students gets old. Kick a kid out and where does he go? The streets, that's where, and the school failed. You can see it coming with a few.

Bobby was from a decent family, but he was one of those who had a particularly mean, reckless streak. Kicked him out, and it wasn't long until he made the FBI's most wanted list.

Some students have nowhere else to go. Melissa, a sophomore, had moved from home to home, school to school. She'd been away somewhere and returned to re-enroll. The counselor who should have re-enrolled her was absent that day.

Come in and have a seat, Melissa.

She was resentful, belligerent, and uncooperative. Talk about a nasty attitude. I decided to go easy with her, thinking maybe she would calm down and open up a bit. She had been living with her grandparents where an uncle beat the girl with the bad attitude. Then she moved back with her alcoholic father, who abused her. He lived with his girlfriend, who had a former boyfriend who showed up one day threatening them with a gun.

I tried to console and encourage her.

Look, Melissa, turn over a new leaf. It might work here this time. Let's give it a try, and if you let me, I'll help, but you have to help yourself, too. Make the most of it. You've got to be someplace, don't you?

Man, there ain't no place to be, she said.

She hung on for a while and then went away.

What could I do, but hope she would find a place?

CHAPTER 12

Moving On Up or Down

On April 16, 1975, a little freshman girl asked, Mr. C, are you going to be our principal next year?

Oh, I don't know. Are you going to be a student next year?

If you are the principal, I will be.

I'm not going to be the principal, because I quit. Why quit, when I've never been a quitter? Always lived life in a cup spilling over, but had put so much into the job that it took too much out of me. It was a day-and-night job, with ballgames on weekends, holidays interrupted, vacations limited. I saw my immediate family on Sundays and my mother not enough. You can't get away from 2,700 students in a home away from home.

I didn't have bleeding ulcers yet, so I thought maybe I should gut it out. A captain of a ship sailing in smooth seas enjoys the ride, but he must use his spyglass to look for storms that wreck and sink ships. When I asked God to give me a break, He said, I didn't give Moses a break.

I decided to move on and up, way up, to a central office where school superintendents lock the door to their offices, and are shielded from live children and ungodly teenagers. That's what I'll do—segregate myself from teachers and students and the things they do to each other and to me. I'll work in an office where I can think, plan, and do paperwork, writing things for teachers to do.

I accepted a position as an assistant superintendent at the South Harrison School Corporation in Corydon, Indiana. Corydon is a small town that was Indiana's first state capital. It's rural, scenic, and an historic area, located only thirty miles from Louisville. A few weeks on the job, a reporter asked how I was adjusting to the new position after years in the trenches. Great if I can adjust to the tranquility, I said.

It was tough to move on and give up what I had worked for with all my heart and soul. And it was tough to see what happened to modular scheduling at PHS and JHS. Both programs died. A principal must understand it, believe in it, and slave away at it. For the most part, both communities accepted and supported the change and supported me. Of course, there were the critics and the politics. The traditionalists could never accept that young people would take more responsibility for their own learning and decide where they wanted to go and what they wanted to do during unscheduled time. Most all of them did their work, but traditionalists thought they should be locked in so we knew exactly what they were doing and where they were.

Students are locked down now, and we know where they are. About two-thirds do what teachers tell them to do, while others sit there dazed, barely making it. And others move on to live in poverty or off the welfare state. A rare few make it once they move out of the nearly insurmountable odds stacked against them. Most societies, industries, and institutions change with the times. Governments and schools remain basically the same.

My responsibilities as assistant superintendent included staffing, the curriculum, and the improvement of instruction. I hired the best teachers I could find and worked to improve the instructional programs in the two high schools and five elementary schools. All my experience had been in secondary education. What did I know about teaching children to read? I began exploring the theories, methods, and practices of teaching reading. Apparently, there is not a foolproof way, but the elementary teachers were enthusiastic and we began to make some progress.

It was peaceful in my safe and secure office. Planning, thinking, and sorting papers doesn't churn your stomach. But I missed the action, so I visited the schools, sat in classes, and made suggestions. Most teachers are too busy to heed suggestions, but they were nice to me, and then I'd go back to the office and sort more papers.

If teaching reading to all children is tough, what about

writing? It's tougher. First, you have to teach pronouns and verbs, and don't forget possessives. I observed a fifth-grade class one day, and the teacher said, You haven't learned your possessives, so we're going to review them today.

A few days later, I observed a senior English class. The teacher said, You haven't learned your possessives, so we're going to review them today. Eight straight years of reviewing possessives is a bit much, don't you think?

During that time, I also taught a graduate class at Indiana University Southeast for teachers and a few others working on their master's degrees. They also wrote papers and, apparently, there are teachers who received a C- in English.

I decided I didn't want to be a superintendent, who does two things—sweat the budget and play politics. Some of them place improving education first, but there are always other fires to put out before working on improving reading scores.

I can't balance my own budget and I hate politics. Politics has no place in religion and education. Preachers spread the word of God to please Him, but you can't please the entire flock all the time. Principals usually try to improve education, with or without God's help, but keeping the lid on the school building comes first.

School board members say they want to improve education, too. Particularly in smaller school systems, the best way to improve is to hire local teachers, bus drivers, cafeteria workers, secretaries, and custodians. We're all family here, and I have a member of my own family who wants to teach or drive a school bus. But you can recommend a non-local basketball coach, if he's a big winner. Winning teachers frequently become lost in the local politics and the bureaucratic maze.

The chairman of the school board had a daughter who had a teaching license, and desperately needed a job. If I didn't recommend her, there'd be a huge price to pay. Of about twenty applicants, the chairman's daughter ranked twenty-first. No way could I recommend her. Think! Here's what I'll do, I'll bundle the five elementary teachers to be hired into two packages. Package #1 did not include the chairman's daughter, but package # 2 did. When the time came for my recommendations to the board, they became tense.

I told the board that I'd searched for the best teachers I could find, and found some good ones, so many in fact that I couldn't make a decision. Look at these two packages, and it will be hard for you, but choose one. Eagerly, they looked about a minute at the two options. A board member then moved to select Package #2, which included the chairman's daughter. It was unanimous. A board member told me afterward, are we ever glad you did it that way.

How was I to know the new, young, dynamic, band teacher might be a lesbian until someone reported seeing her walking through a secluded wooded park holding the hand of junior girl band member? The chairman of the board called a mass meeting. Preachers and their faithful lined up on one side and the band parents lined up on the opposite side. Their children had been playing terribly off key until the new band teacher arrived and had them marching down streets to the beat of powerful drums. In this community where God lived, it was determined that the music teacher certainly knew how to lead a band and she kept her job.

In another instance, a chairman of the school board permitted two of his sons to drop out of school. Since when does a farmer or hired hand need a high school diploma?

The kids were giving a bus driver fits. The board called the driver in, and each board member explained in depth how they would handle the kids if they drove the bus. Why else were they elected to the board? In many school systems, large or small, coaches, buses, and cafeterias take precedence over the improvement of education.

Education gets bogged down almost everywhere. It starts with federal and state department bureaucracies loaded with so-called education experts who become political appointees. Our nation talks about improving education, but many decisions involving schools become entangled in politics. Try passing a referendum raising taxes to support schools.

I didn't want to play politics with school boards, and decided to move on after two years of decaying in a gloomy office where students, teachers, parents, and cranks weren't beating on my door. I went back to where the action was, where our future lies—inside the minds of America's youth.

I accepted a position as an assistant principal at Floyd Central High School in Floyd County, Indiana. I went from the captain of a ship to swabbing the decks, and went down the prestige ladder. Why? The higher up you go on the rungs of a status ladder, the greater the danger of falling off. When you land—splat. The change also provided more time to get to know my family and the buck stopped somewhere else, which provided the opportunity to go home at night and get some sleep.

I also had six weeks off in the summer, which provided time to do a few things I'd always wanted to do—see part of the world and maybe try writing something.

Back in the Line of Fire and Brimstone

The Bible warns of being consumed by fire and brimstone. God sent both to burn and destroy Sodom and Gomorrah, including their high schools. And there I was back in the fire at Floyd Central High School, located about twenty minutes from downtown Louisville. It is in a scenic rural setting, on a plateau known as the Knobs. The school had about 1,000 students, but since then has grown to about 1,600 students. As the suburban area grew, business and professional people moved into the area, which strengthened the academic programs. Educated parents demand good schools. If you have children and are moving, drive around the area and look at the homes. Higher-cost homes are a reliable indicator of the quality of the schools. Also, look at the percentage of the students receiving free lunch. Generally, those schools in a low socio-economic area struggle. Why can't the bad schools catch up with the good ones? Children and youth from families living in projects, low-rent homes or apartments, and/or unstable families generally have low self-esteem, low expectations, and low achievement, and are often malnourished. School is not a priority; existence and TV are. Although, FCHS is located in a somewhat higher socio-economic area, the issues and problems are basically the same in all schools. Parents, teachers, and kids do stupid things wherever they live.

At FCHS, my title was director of student development. I directed students toward development, but they will develop whether you direct them or not. We also had a director of staff development. The staff thought they had already developed and didn't want to be bothered.

I tried developing Judy, who was having extreme anxiety in her driver education class. Her teacher was, too, and when she was out practicing driving one day, her teacher instructed her to pull over and stop. She hit the brakes, causing him to lurch forward. He had to run into a store for something—perhaps coffee to settle his nerves. When he did, Judy lit a cigarette, puffing rapidly to settle her nerves.

Judy, you know you can't smoke in school.

I wasn't in school. I was in a car.

The car is a part of school property, you know?

But I was halfway in and halfway out; it shouldn't count.

You can't be halfway in and halfway out of a school or anything in life. It's all or nothing.

There I was, completely back in the hearts, minds, and souls of America's nervous and anxious youth.

Judy, I know you are nervous. I've been there, too. Although school may appear dim inside, the future can be bright for you outside. If life is a drag for you at sixteen, think twenty-six. Think responsibilities such as parenting. Will you want your children smoking inside or outside a car?

No, I won't, because I'll love them as soon as I can have one.

Will you be nervous and smoke around them?

No, because I don't plan to be as nervous then.

To direct students to full development, you have to get inside their heads to see what they are up to and what's going on in there. I thought I'd seen it all, but I saw things before my eyes that had never occurred before in human history, including forty-one snakes slithering around the locker area just before school dismissed after another exciting day.

Before the forty-one snakes, I'd caught five live chickens clucking through the school. Before that, toward the end of their senior year, the class of '75 at JHS planned to bring a horse inside the school, but brought a pig instead. I heard shouting and squealing. The half-grown pig, with "Class of '75" painted on both sides, ran excitedly through our school with a herd of seniors eagerly following. I picked up the pig as if it were a piece of trash, which I also did when taking a leisurely walk through our lovely school. The seniors cheered as we marched through the halls. Teachers who were teaching became alarmed at the squealing, but it amounted to nothing—all in a day's work. From a photograph, a highly talented art student painted a Picasso-type work of Mr. C and His Pig. It's one of my prized possessions.

Raymond, the snake handler, had never caused any problems before. During the afternoons, he went to his building-trades class site to learn how to build a house. It was springtime and raining torrents, flooding part of the backyard of the house he was building. Raymond looked out and saw snakes, gobs of them escaping from their winter hibernation nests. He had a gym bag handy, perfect for capturing the forty-one cold, bewildered serpents. How did I know there were forty-one? Honest Raymond told me; he counted them.

Upon returning to FCHS to catch a bus home, he went to his locker to get some things, but before he could put books in his gym bag, he had to do something with the forty-one snakes writhing and coiling inside his gym bag. Why not pour them out on the locker-area floor just before the bell rang? He did. Screaming, blood-curdling mayhem followed. What a shock to reach for an English grammar book, but pick up a foot-long garter snake.

After the students sprinted to their buses, I announced a Code Red alert, ordering the custodial staff to stop cleaning until they captured all forty-one snakes. To this day, it's possible that twenty-two snakes—perhaps as long as Burmese pythons by now—lie coiled somewhere in the rafters of FCHS.

Give the young credit for being creative.

I've witnessed many violations of strict school laws. A justice system deals with crime and punishment, and I'm the chief justice, determining penalties or pardons. A student who is repeatedly tardy must be punished according to established law. But like Congress, a school can't pass enough laws to cover everything. I couldn't imprison them, but some thought they were already trapped in solitary confinement.

I tried everything: Expulsion (no other choice for the hard core); suspension from school, up to five days; detention and community service, which worked but was too unwieldy.

In-school suspension was better than out-of-school suspension. Parents knew where their children were. We had a room supervised by a monitor. Students couldn't talk and had to work on their assignments sent by their teachers. To calm them, I piped classical music into the room—Mozart and Bach. One student said that he could accept in-school suspension, but not that kind of music, which drove him nuts. One girl said, Please assign me there for the rest of the year, because I will goof off in the classrooms and I want to graduate.

Why not assign themes to those committing misdemeanors?

You're suspended or write a 500-, 750- or a 1,000-word theme depending on the severity of the crime, similar to the penalty for jaywalking or reckless driving. Write about

My Responsibility or My Future or My Family or Why I Did What I Did.

To complete the assignment, a student had to sit down and think. Then I had to think when I read what they wrote. When I called the student back in, we both tried to think. When they wrote about My Family, I often thought, with a family like that, I'd be locked up.

When students violated class procedures, disturbed class, or acted out, teachers needed to take action. Kicking them out of class didn't solve the problem; it only created other problems. What could a teacher do? We developed a demerit system. Teachers filled out a student development form, stating the violation, and they could assign demerits. When a student accumulated a certain number of demerits, things happened, perhaps a day of in-school suspension or a parent conference. A student could also repent of their sins by working off their demerits with the teacher, and then that student-teacher relationship became all lovely again.

Here are some statements frustrated teachers wrote on student development forms:

Joey hit Brad in the face with a rubber chicken about five times.

Travis carried the brain of a crayfish around the room shoving it under girls' noses.

Danny disturbed class with a fart-gas can.

Brian locked the substitute teacher out of the room.

Ryan tried to put Wayne in a garbage can.

Jim put mustard on Bruce who rubbed it on Troy who then poured milk on Bruce's head.

Joey meowed like a cat.

John barked like a dog when I asked for his assignment.

Junior said, your anus, to another student in science class, said anus is a scientific word.

Scott cut class, said his ulcer reacted to the school lunch.

During third period, Chris played with a hopping toy penis.

In explaining two lines in Hamlet, Louis said it gets me hard.

Sammy rubbed Connie's thighs during orchestra class.

Robert tickled a girl so hard she wet her pants.

Matt brought a frog liver to class.

Rick passed gas loudly. Told him to take Gas-X or get demerits.

Sandra said Jesus and had been warned the last two days not to say Jesus.

It's better to say Jesus than to take the Lord's name in vain. (If you say Jesus one more time, I will not turn my other cheek.) There was a time when students—and teachers—didn't dare use bad words. Not anymore. This school sucks or f__k this class is commonplace. Some teachers overlook it and some don't. I gave up trying to get students and teachers to refrain from saying vain or harsh words listed in the Bible and the dictionary.

I've-had-it teachers frequently sent students to the office without an explanation.

Rick, why are you here? Write the truth on this paper.

He wrote: I casually entered the room at the proper time with the necessary materials to complete the class. At approximately 12:58, I had the urge to have a vowel movement. (They had been studying vowels and consonants.) I kept it inside but slowly it built up to where I could not retain it. So, I asked the teacher for a pass, but she would not give it to me. I begged and pleaded with her.

Some teachers know precisely when students need to use the bathroom. How they know this, I do not know.

Eric, why did you steal four bags of potato chips from the cafeteria? Address dishonesty on this paper.

I think dishonesty is very disrespectful and not very honest at all. It can move into things like cars and people's houses. Stealing is one of the commandments it is the 6th one. I am also a catholic and go to church on Sundays and religion on Wednesdays. That is a very bad sin to God. I will probably go to confecsion to tell I have sinned. That makes me pretty mad when I think what I did.

Wayne explained why he shouldn't chew gum: It's sticky and after you chew it a while, it loses its flavor. Another reason is that teachers watch you to see if your mouth is moving.

Margie wrote in part: My grandpa steals wine, because he's a wino. My mother is not sure who my dad is, but if he is my dad, he's in prison. My mom ran with the Hell's Angels until they robbed a store and now she's in prison. Last week, uncle Dallas went to prison because he killed a man. That's all for now.

That was enough.

Jesse wrote: I don't have a positive attitude about the future. Guess I'll live on the streets and go in the drug business. Cocaine is a good thing to invest in and a good profit.

Carrie wrote: Mr. Cummins, I'm really sorry about fighting Heather this morning. I apologized to her while we were waiting for you. And I apologize to you for getting you involved. Love ya honestly, Carrie.

I love you, too, Carrie, honestly.

Nicole ran away from home and wrote about it: I have learned a lot from all the trouble I've been in. I learned that many people care about me like my parents, friends, police, the youth shelters, my school, and my probation officers. I also learned how much an education matters in life. It has helped me set goals and reach for the stars.

Nicole began reaching for the stars when she returned home and re-entered school.

Willie wrote about his future. He wanted to buy land in Canada near a lake, build a cabin with a hot tub, and live the good life. (After reading the description of his cabin, I'd move there, too.) Willie also wrote: I don't know if you really care about all this, but I'm glad someone knows what I want. This is the first time I have ever brought this out in the open, because no one else seems to care what anybody wants in life. There are so many things still a little fuzzy for me, but I'm beginning to figure out what I want in life. I've just put down what was on my mind. I do this every once in a while. Could I have this back or a copy of it before I leave school? It's part of a little diary-type bunch of papers I write.

Willie, you can have it back if you promise to follow your dreams.

David wrote that the way to avoid a fight was to avoid the stress that comes before it. Stress for me is the confusion created when one does not override the body's desire to choke the daylights out of a person who desperately needs it.

In the 1960s, boys had to wear their shirttails inside their trousers.

Ronald, write about why you wore your shirttail out.

I have no particular reason for wearing it out except girls do and my shirt hurts my side if it is in. What are some reasons for wearing shirttails in?

I couldn't think of any, or why long hair is evil.

Dealing with kids who brought frog livers to class, passed gas, or said Jesus was easy; the tough ones were not. A teacher said, my students told me Jeff is at home and said he's going to kill himself. I immediately called Jeff's mom at work, and she rushed home. They got help for Jeff, and a few weeks later he returned to school and did well.

The word spread that an irate father with a gun was on

the way to school. I met him at the front door, and if he had a gun, I didn't see it.

Come in and let's talk. He did and settled down.

Danny, why don't you like school?

I like school when the teachers put some action in it, but I don't like it when all they do is assign and tell us to do our work. I would like to be taught things with some spirit in it.

Jackie said: I like school. It's pretty fun once you get someone who cares about you.

Hugh said: Like for instance, I think school is sometimes boring. I don't mean boring as if I don't care, but I mean as the teachers don't explain as I like them to put in some light.

Don't we all want some light put in it?

Randy wrote: All I ask of this school is let me take a class that I can pass.

Sheila wrote: When I was three and my sister five, my mom decided to take us to our grandmother's house, and she never came back.

What do you say to Randy, who wants only a class he can pass, or to Sheila, whose mom never came back?

All schools have a few students like Pete. He was a very good student, never a problem, but kind of lost it with a teacher one day.

Okay, Pete, write 500 words on proper public behavior. His take on public behavior stemmed from Plato, as he explained:

The subject of public behavior has been queried by many of the world's greatest philosophers. Plato believed that we owe our total existence to society. Jean-Paul Sartre believed we owe no more to society than it owes to us. He also believed that an individual should do what he wants and to hell with society. Coming to our encounter yesterday in the corridor, I was under emotional stress and extremely nervous. I have been under unusual pressure and feel as though I'm being deceived, that I'm not getting it straight. I feel as though I'm being treated as if I were twelve. The attitude most students are adopting is, if I'm going to be treated as a child, I shall act like one.

At the follow-up conference, Pete and I talked Plato, Sartre, stress, and pressure. Pete, you won't have to put up with this Mickey Mouse stuff much longer and I'm a part of it, but telling society to go hell won't work for you. When you leave here, you have something valuable to offer, and I hope you will.

His paper allowed him to release some of his frustrations, and I appreciated his helping clarify Sartre's philosophy for me.

Unlike Pete, Larry had developed his own life philosophy and also wrote about public behavior using capital letters for emphasis and spelled words the way they sound—the way it should be:

Cussing is one of the most unpolite things one can do. It inter ups the class and it degrades you in Honor and Respect. Do not Pillage the books in school or anywhere else. Do not! Steal do not Sabotage the desks, the Black Board and the teachers seat. Do not throw things or fly things. You should not spit tobacco on the floor or the walls. You ought to lesson to your teachers they can be helpful sometimes. Do not give up on yourself, your teachers, your parents or giardian. Think of other people when you do anything at all.

That's good Larry, thinking of other people. I'm thinking about you right now and don't want you to give up on yourself.

I often think of Sheila, Larry, and the other young people facing tremendous odds. Schools are geared to those who can succeed. For those who struggle, how do they endure? As Jackie said, School is pretty fun once you find someone who cares.

And then there are students like Chris, who gave his teachers fits. He wrote: I've been having a lot of problems that I don't really know how to handle and really can't talk to anyone about. It just seems like my dream of becoming a Marine is falling apart. I mess up everything. I'm just a foul up. I guess I'll never be a Marine.

His bus driver said he was the only monkey on his bus. His lady English teacher, whom he had driven up the wall, had been in the Air Force.

Chris, it's not too late. All you need to do is shape up, and not give up. I believe you can do it. He did shape up, barely making it through graduation. About six months later, Chris walked in, his Marine uniform spotless, shoes and buckles glistening.

During the Vietnam War, Billy sent two long letters to me explaining the hellish fighting he was in. Said he was okay, but wondered if I was okay. I wrote back: Thanks for your letters, Billy, they mean a lot to me. I'm okay, but take good care of yourself and make sure to come see me when you return.

I was okay until he was killed in action a few months later.

If one believes in the young and wants to see them all succeed, it's difficult to avoid becoming bound up in their lives. Giving one's all is draining and eventually takes a toll. But even as these difficult and trying human-relation conflicts and situations evolve and transpire, 90 percent of the rooms are filled with bright, eager students learning from capable and involved teachers. Their creative shenanigans can be dealt with, but that sizeable portion of seemingly I-don't-care young people tests one's will and resolve. Once they believe in someone they respect, who truly cares, they have a much greater chance of becoming successful, and finding happiness ever after—up to a point.

CHAPTER 14

How Did That Ever Enter Your Mind?

Teenage minds amaze me. Soon after they wake up, their minds begin twirling and filling with thoughts, some of them abnormal. When students board the school buses early each morning, they are usually dazed and dozing, but get somewhat wildish in the afternoons with pent-up nervous energy and hormones racing, often talking dirty, and then touching, pushing, pinching, rubbing, and squealing.

Not many school bus drivers take psychology courses or have had instruction in promoting warm human relations. After a school day, a loaded school bus taking children back home is often like a farmer taking nervous cattle to a slaughterhouse. I had situations where the bus driver departed school, then turned the bus around, returned to school, and sent for me to come quickly to restore order.

Gentle Charlie sent in a bus infraction report that read: Tina threw a condom with hand lotion in it at her driver.

Tina, did you throw it?

I threw it at Tony and missed.

When Big Fred told Rooky to sit on the front seat of the bus, Rooky said: I ain't sitting on no front seat. Big Fred put a headlock on him and dragged him to the front seat. Rooky's dad called and said he'd kill Big Fred, but he didn't.

Each day on Jake's bus, immoral students openly discussed subjects such as fornication or sex with animals. Righteous parents became alarmed. After a thorough investigation, it was determined that Jake turned off his hearing aid when he drove, wanting to concentrate on the road, and not be distracted by loud noises or sexually related conversations.

Students discover sex in junior high and then conduct experiments with it in high school, similar to conducting experiments in science or cooking classes. Not all students are knowledgeable or sophisticated about sex. Not knowing that his teacher was listening, Thad, a freshman, explained what he thought oral sex was after another freshman said it was when you get the phone number at Playboy and call them up. Thad said, for all to hear, no, it was when you use your mouth.

His teacher then said, Thad, go stand in the hall. When he did, the teacher next door quickly opened his door, hitting Thad in the head, knocking him down and nearly out. Alarmed, the teacher brought Thad to my office with a large bump on his head.

What happened, Thad?

Nothing really. (They all say that.)

As time passed, clothing became skimpier to the point where students began letting it all hang out. Schools were then forced to adopt dress codes regarding what and how much could hang out. Committees were formed, and students had input. In one English class, the teacher asked her students to write what a dress code should include. The students offered some excellent points, indicating that our young support morality as it relates to nudity:

Shorts shouldn't be worn too tightly and gripping the body. Boys should not wear pants with holes that show the personals.

I think the reason girls wear halter-tops is probably because they are hot.

How can a T-shirt with, Bite My Big Toe, sprawled across the front reflect one's individuality?

Tight clothes cut off circulation and the student might pass out.

Short is ok as long as organisms don't hang out.

Take any boy with hormones and put him in a room with a girl and he's bound to keep his mind on the skirts that seem to be painted on. So while he's trying to look up that skirt how much will he learn that day? Nothing I tell you!

Yes, nothing, I tell you, but learning is important in a school. We must eliminate extraneous distractions. When a principal is distracted, he should re-focus. The future of America depends on it.

Special education students are truly special. Before the 1960s, young people with various handicaps were kept at home. School was no place for those who couldn't learn. And then we realized that all had a right to an education. I started the first special class at PHS. What will those students learn? They will learn that they are important, and can become a part of the school and society. Special education students require an extraordinary amount of patience and understanding, which successful special education teachers possess. They are a special breed. Those students with emotional and psychological problems can test the limits of how far one's patience can go.

There are many success stories. David had all kinds of problems, emotional and physical, and he struggled to fit in. But those who worked with him never gave up. Amazingly, he made it through high school and college. I went to his wedding and now he's happy working in a government office.

Special education students are compassionate, considerate, and most appreciative of those who give special care. One special girl summed up their needs as she kept singing, What the world needs now is love, sweet love. Often when I felt a bit down, I'd visit a special ed class, and they'd be so happy for the attention. And I'd be happy for the good-natured strength they revealed to me.

Let's not forget that ballgames are as important as English, math, and any other thing a high school imparts. In Kentucky and Indiana, basketball reigns supreme and winning teams take precedence over the economy, religion, and SAT scores. Jeffersonville High and neighboring New Albany High had been bitter rivals since the turn of the twentieth century. JHS didn't defeat NAHS in football until 1974. The battles were as fierce as those of the North and South in the 1860s.

When JHS finally won, I feared for the safety of the people in Southern Indiana. In the old days, fans rioted in the streets, and in one instance, turned a streetcar over.

At the basketball games, up to five thousand rabid fans, as in mad dogs, packed the gyms, screaming for blood. What could be in their minds? JHS students painted SONA signs (Sh_t on New Albany), posted them on the streets and chanted SONA, SONA, at the games.

The NAHS principal and I worked hard to bring civility to our communities. At one critical basketball game, our cheerleaders planned to host the NAHS cheerleaders by providing a hospitality room for them with brownies, fruit, and drinks.

That is a very nice and thoughtful thing to do in the spirit of promoting sportsmanship and intra-school relations, I said to our perky cheerleaders.

Early the next Monday morning, the NAHS principal called. He said his cheerleaders became sick after the game and one went to the hospital. He consulted with the doctor, and said to me: Apparently, your cheerleaders put Ex-Lax in the brownies.

They sure did.

A principal might work to the bone during the week, but he had to attend the big games on Friday night and maybe another one on Saturday night, seventy-five miles away. On many Fridays, I arrived at school at seven a.m. and was not back home until around midnight. Years of it wore me out.

In addition to the packed gym, the cafeteria gave me heartburn, indigestion, and queasy feelings. It wasn't the food; it was when they threw it.

Word got out there would be a big food fight the next day: Oh, my God. We waited, but all was calm, and then two boys from a drama class ran to the cafeteria and began wrestling and throwing punches. One was dressed as a cereal box and the other as a can of pork and beans. Deep inside a principal's consciousness is the eternal question: What will they think of next?

I ate lunch with the students to be friendly and kept one eye peeled. During one nice lunch, I sat beside a teacher who said, Look over there; the senior class president is drunk. He was. It's a long story, but I want to get back to learning and teaching and maybe check on a shaky substitute teacher.

Teachers get sick, physically and mentally, and when they do substitute teachers have the hardest jobs in the world. No one can substitute for a teacher. A student came to my office and said, You should go to room 203. The sub teacher is sitting in there smoking.

You can't smoke in here, I said.

Stubbing the cigarette out, he said, Sorry, I'm so nervous.

Make that two of us, I said.

In a nearby high school, a sub teacher asked the class if anyone had a joint. A girl said yes, and the sub teacher lit up. In another nearby high school, a teacher stopped by the office and a bag of marijuana accidently dropped out of his pocket. One teacher kept a bottle of wine in her desk. When her students went to lunch, she locked the door and relaxed. Stress gets to a teacher around noon. Not that many teachers are winos. Professional ones get high when their students do well.

I observed the increasing number of deeply disturbed students, beginning in the 1980s. Who knew what they were thinking? A few thought, for whatever reason, that no one paid attention to them, no one understood them, and no one cared about them.

The preps and the jocks and the goody-goodies make me sick.

Authority makes me sicker.

I know how I can get their attention in a big way. They'll look at me when I walk in dressed in a long dark coat.

It's always safety first in schools, but guns are not safe. On three occasions, we took guns from students after other students passed the word. Through the years, there were isolated instances of school officials being shot. In the dark of night, someone shot a bullet through the front of the home of our dean of boys. A fellow principal and good friend had an armed student hold a classroom hostage one afternoon. They eventually talked him down.

Later, massacres occurred at Columbine and several other schools. Potential assassins exist in every high school, and that thought stays tucked away in every principal's consciousness.

Fire smoldered in Edward's eyes. He was quiet and reserved, but wrapped in a bundle of nerves. He resented people telling him what to do and thought the world was against him. He was one of the potentials who could go off. It took several talks to bring him down. Edward, you've got to learn to put up with some of the stuff in your life. We all do. Come and talk to me when you get too tight, will you? His eyes cleared a bit, and he began to realize the world and the school was not against him.

There wasn't enough time to work with all the disturbed kids, but giving some time to those who needed it most indicated that I did care. Edward turned himself around.

CHAPTER 15

The Things within Me

I had many things within me back then, and those still exist, but I did not have as many things in me as Sandra had in her, and she'd just turned sixteen. The things within her became another thing within me, to the extent I wrote a twenty-three-page account about our ensuing drama.

Sandra had been skipping school and was assigned a 1,000-word theme, which she titled "The Things Within Me." It was one of the more hostile, scathing, and vulgar themes I'd ever read from a student. A conference was arranged with her counselor and parents.

Her parents appeared decent, but were obviously uncomfortable. They were some of those she's-driving-us-crazy parents. I had not remembered talking to Sandra before, but remembered talking to her boyfriend, John, also sixteen.

He came in one day to explain why he'd missed school.

Said he had to take Sandra to the doctor to see if she was pregnant. We had a kind of father-son talk.

John, do you know what contraception is?

Yeah, but I took a chance.

He didn't believe in abortion and assured me he and Sandra could meet the awesome responsibilities ahead and live happily ever after. He also confided that another girl accused him of getting her pregnant, but he said he was drunk at the time and could never do anything when he was drunk.

John had been an abused child, was a ward of the court, and had bounced from one foster home to another. His deep-seated hostility and aggression finally got the best of him and he was expelled from school.

At Sandra's conference, she sat there defiant, with daggers in her eyes. I explained that she hadn't been doing her schoolwork and had been skipping school. I'd assigned her a theme to confess and repent of her sins. I held up her theme and said, these are some of the things she wrote.

I skipped school because I didn't feel like going and had other things to do and people to see—this stupid school sucks—my mother bitches all the time—my boyfriend loves me long as he gets in my pants—this school is for preps not for other people cause we don't kiss ass and never will—you all expect us to respect you when you treat us like s__t.

Sandra included other scathing statements, but she also wrote: You know I like to write poems. I write you a few here and you can see if you like them or not and see if I got a talent in it or not.

When I mentioned she'd included her poems, Sandra jumped up, went behind me, pointed to her theme, and said, I wrote this one and that one and I added this one about what is a family. She described a family as: A source of joy and laughter, jokes and secrets, smiles and tears, and a wealth of treasures. She also included this line: Parents often think about the younger generation as if they had nothing to do with it. Her poems and dream also included this line: Love is like a road that never ends: It always seems to keep running to you.

This girl, who was passing only two of her classes at the time with a D and a D-, was spending way too much time writing poetry.

I told Sandra to re-write her 1,000-word theme and turn it in the following Monday, and we would go from there. Thanks for coming in, I said.

No, I'll have it for you tomorrow, she said.

That same day, I talked to Faye. She was fifteen and had about every pitiful problem imaginable. Among other things, she'd been skipping school, too. I assigned her a theme about her family.

Faye wrote: My home life is bizarre, but that's just the way things are. My mother had three children before she was 19. My dad doesn't care if we go out and kill someone. My mother is married for the second time, but she lives with another man part time, who is married but doesn't live with his wife.

Faye, you mean these people aren't divorced?

They get divorced sometimes, but they live like this until they get in a big fight. Mommy mixed up all our lives.

Faye's doctor's office had called the school earlier and asked that she call his office. It was urgent that she see her doctor today, they said, because her baby might be in the wrong place.

I'll see she gets there, I said. Maybe mixed-up Mommy will take her.

What is this, unwed mother's day? All these things disrupt school. Sex education doesn't work; poetry education doesn't work. Dissecting frogs, yuck. What works best is a good home.

The next morning, Sandra dropped off her revision of "The Things Within Me." I sent for her later in the day. As she sat down, her demeanor changed to one of confidence and self-assurance. She showed no defiance as she curiously gazed at me, awaiting my direction.

Sorry, but I've not had time to read this yet, so I'll read it aloud now and we'll talk about it if need be. Her eyes seemed to ask, please listen to the things within me:

I know the things I wrote about school wasn't true, at least most of them anyway.

She did raise one concern, the kids known as preppies or

preps: I guess it's cuz they do everything they're supposed to do and don't goof around like some of us do. And then: No trouble good kid that's the real me. The last few weeks hasn't been the real me and I know I need to change. I wrote a poem I want you to read:

Life is strang!
I wish it would chang!
The Drugs and Stuff!
Its all to ruff!
Pretty soon the world will
Come to an End!
There wont be any one to turn lights on

Obviously, she needed help with her spelling and punctuation. I thought, I'll talk to her English teacher. No, I'll keep talking to her.

I wrote it today, and I wrote another one during third period I want you to read, she said.

It was a love poem describing her feelings about loneliness, love, and longing for and crying over a faraway lover. I feel like I'm dying, she wrote.

I don't have time to sit here reading poetry. If I had time for poetry, I'd read Dickinson or Frost.

Here's one more I wrote during seventh period:

I'm settin here!
And Nothing is to clear!
But I'm working it out!
I'll probably let out a shout!
Everything seems cloudy!

I'm glad I'm not rowdy!
Well guess I better go!
So my work will show!

Maybe I'm not wasting my time reading her poems; they were an outlet for what was inside her. I looked up and smiled at her: Keep writing these poems, and you should probably write a few of your English class assignments, too. She smiled back.

Then I read aloud:

I guess it's just I was hurt about Tommy and Billy and I took it out on the school.

A couple of weeks before, Tommy was killed in a car wreck and Billy took his own life shortly thereafter.

She wrote: Tommy had been very close and used to go with my best friend and he was like a brother to me. I wish he had been smart and not taken that car. It hurts when one of your best friends gets killed. I used to go with Billy for about a year and then he quit school and we decided to give up our relationship.

She proceeded to give an account of the funerals and particularly made note of the friends who attended: You know you don't really know who you friends are till after your dead.

I made some comment to her and noticed the tears returning, although she was trying to remain composed.

Billy said on that tape he left that he had no friends, had no money, and no place to go, so what's the reason for living. If he could have been there to see all the people there, he would have been surprised.

She addressed the question or concept of caring several times. In a sense, the underlying theme of her paper was does anyone really care about me?

After the poems, the remainder of the reading took only a couple of minutes, while the intensity of my emotions and feelings for her thickened the lump in my throat and blurry drips covered my eyes. She sat there with a concealed strength. Her resolve and courage seemed to defy the tears that fell as she described her lengthy conversation with Billy on a Friday two days before he took his life.

And I told him I still cared a great deal about him, and that I would always take him back. He goes thanks but everything is okay but he didn't look okay he looked puzzled.

After previously attacking and blasting me, she had now conquered and reduced me. I had been consumed by the force of an aching, wounded heart of a young lady with too many things within her that had to come out.

Then I told Billy remember I care and I'm always here for you.

I stopped reading: Sandra, do you believe I care?

She spontaneously nodded yes as she looked at me with conviction. The pause that bound that moment seemed to make the world—our world—one of peace, sealed from all the externals, a moment of unexplainable, but irrevocable solace.

I had only a few more lines to read before the last bell would ring and she would leave. I stared at the words, forcing them out:

He goes thanks and Happy Birthday if I don't see you. And they ended up finding him on my birthday.

They found him on her birthday! I did not read aloud the last line of her things within me. It was: God life is weird.

In silence, I think each of us understood more about that which is weird, while at the same time, also agreeing, as she had written in her first theme, that love is like a road that never ends.

You have to go now. Will you come and talk to me next week?

Yes, she said as she left the room.

This sixteen-year-old, academically achieving at a very low level, was so weak and vulnerable. And yet, she was also strong and bold and filled with the substance of life, perplexing as that may be, and she had the expectancy of— love always seems to keep running at you, but:

Life is strang!

I wish it would chang!

Such are the things within a school.

But I must go now; I've got more school work to do.

CHAPTER 16

The Celebration

I have one large folder in my collection of notes and trash that I haven't mentioned. It's important that I do, and it's labeled Thank You. Only a fragment of the papers, notes, and accounts of the strange, weird, and wonderful things students, parents, and teachers wrote to me or did for me—or to me—have been included in this book.

In times of strife and stress, I'd get letters, notes, and calls—often the same old complaints and concerns, but on occasion, a few surprises. I would be amiss if I failed to acknowledge the folder stuffed with thank-yous for something I had said or done. Those notes, letters, cards, and calls challenged me to continue saying and doing things that might make a difference in someone's life. A thank-you made a difference in mine.

Bobby wrote, Thanks for coming to our class to talk about school and what you do with people's money. Chris said thanks for letting me stay in school. Kathy wrote, Thanks for taking the time to come and talk about values.

Maybe something I said might have prevented someone from doing something foolish. Larry wrote, Thanks for helping me out, I think you are the first person to really understand me.

Teachers are creative and write nice thank-you notes sometimes. Miss Smith expressed her thanks: Thank you for letting us bring the doggy in for the large group session in psychology. It seemed to work very well, and I truly believe that the elements of operant conditioning will be better understood than if I lectured them.

Thank you, Miss Smith. Glad the doggy explained operant conditioning.

Dedicated English teachers occasionally express thanks in poetic fashion. Mrs. Morris composed a poem and wrote it on a nice Hallmark card with a clown-like devil on the front:

Sleepers and Sluggers
Dopers and Muggers
Pushers and Skippers
Book Losers and Trippers
Desk Carvers and Talkers
Constant Lovers and Hall Walkers
Card Bettors and Fire Setters
Carpet Cutters and Bomb Threateners
You Managed To Find Them All
And What's More, Placed Them
All In My Study Hall

What a principal does is talk and talk until his face turns bluish, red, or burnt orange. He tries to convince young people to see the light that illuminates the way. They don't want to hear it, but they do. They are impressionable, and I never knew when something I said might make a difference.

I didn't have time to sit and think much, because I also had to talk to students, teachers, and parents to calm them down. If I could calm them before they got too excited, then I could stop and think about what I was actually doing, and hope that one or two of them were listening. Through vast experience, I devised an Excitement Law, which says that if humans of any age and any IQ can become excited about anything, they will. It's a law of diminished expectations and a law of bewildering complications.

To correct, inspire, or calm them, I'd go talk to each English class a couple of times a year to let all the students know that principals are humans, too, and that my calling was to help them remain calm during times of frustration— whether over grammar, a wayward girlfriend, or dissecting a frog.

In one class, a boy asked, Whose side are you on?

Glad you asked. The reason I'm here is that I'm on your side. If you weren't here, I wouldn't have a job.

Some of the things I said to them as they squirmed: Each person in this room is of equal importance, and everyone is very important. Your rank in class has nothing to do with your importance. If you are at the bottom, your importance ranks up there with the valedictorian. (He doesn't mean that, does he?) Perhaps you young people are more important than your teachers and me. We've lived more life than you have. You're just getting started with your life and have a lot more decisions to make. Your future depends on what you decide. You have decided or will decide how you react to this school. If you're not doing well, only you can make a change. Whatever you do, get through this school. It won't be all fun, but you'll have more fun later. Having money doesn't guarantee happiness, but barely getting by is not the way to go. You've been told that a high school graduate makes a couple of hundred thousand dollars more over a life time than a dropout. A college graduate rakes in considerably more than that. You can be successful and happy without a college degree, if you learn how to work at something the world needs.

Good health is important to me, and your health will be, too, as you grow older. Don't let your friends talk you into swallowing harmful things. I think you know what I mean. One year, seven of our boys were killed in car wrecks. It was a terrible year. Be as careful as you can, because your life is too precious to take unnecessary chances. One of the most important decisions you'll ever make is about taking a chance on bringing a child into the world. Whatever you do, make sure you're ready for that. I live everyday with the stupid mistakes I've made. Your teacher here makes few mistakes, and she knows you need to know what Emily Dickinson knew. Miss Emily wrote about the beautiful things in her life. Try it sometime; it works.

What I do know is that I want all of you to do well. And I do know that your potential is more than what you might think. I know, because I've seen so many young people accomplish so much, and I've seen others just mess around. Don't mess your life around and around. You can't accomplish much when you're dizzy.

There's one thing I want you to do. I do it when I don't know what to do. I talk to other people—young or old—who might be able to help me. Young people have a different perspective on life than older people, who are often set in their ways. Their ways are not always the best ways.

I learned from the young, not just from the brainy types, but maybe more from those who have had a harder way to go.

I'd say, if something really bugs you, talk to someone who might help you. You can always come and talk to me anytime. Believe it or not, it's my job to change your frown into a smiley face. And remember this, if your life has not been what you'd hoped for, you'll soon be out of here and on your own. You can then build the life you want. That's why you should do the best you can in school. Without at least a basic education, your future will be limited. You only have a year or two until you're free from parents and teachers telling you what to do, and from there, about seventy more years to go. What you do now prepares you for all that will come. What kind of life will you choose?

Sorry to disrupt your class, but thanks for allowing me to talk with you. I'd stick around if I had time, because I'd like to hear your teacher explain what Miss Emily meant when she wrote:

This is my letter to the world,
That never wrote me,
The simple news that Nature told,
With tender majesty.

What was the simple news that Nature told? Nature told me to bring some good news to young people. It was not always with tender majesty, but I tried not to waiver from what I chose to do. It was all about teaching and learning in the sacred classroom. I will take credit for trying to eliminate the circus atmosphere, the three rings—clowning around, animal taming, and death-defying high-wire acts. If it's not the greatest show on earth, it's close.

As God warned his small flock at the time of the forbidden fruit, I warned students of the evils of excessive tardiness and dangerous substances that could be ingested or inhaled. One day after groggy students went to their first class, Mr. Harmon, a psychology teacher, sent word that Bill smelled like marijuana. I sent for Bill, closed the door, and sniffed him. Either my nasal passages were clogged, or Bill was innocent. Sorry Bill, someone said you smelled like pot. You don't smoke it, do you?

Oh, no, but maybe you should smell Jake in psych class.

Thanks. I sent for Jake, and when he came through the door, the pot smell about knocked me over. When I called his mother, she rushed over, and furiously got up in Jake's face. Why do you smoke that stuff?

To get high, he said.

That happened in early January, the day after the long holiday break. That same day, it was reported that Matt smelled something like rum. I checked him out, and he told me it was Bacardi rum that he'd poured into a Christmas-present army canteen. On that first day back from break, Matt picked up Bettye, and they sat in the parking lot, guzzling Christmas Bacardi from an army canteen. How else could they muster the courage to go back to school? After two weeks of Christmas merriment and cheer, returning to school and the grind was like going to the parking lot outside hell. From one continuous party to great literature, which nobody reads, to equations and gerunds, to the Revolutionary War, to mutilating dead frogs, and their only means of escaping was to get kite-high, or ask for a restroom pass.

You might think I was like a ringmaster in a circus after reading the stuff I included in this book. I didn't include most of the teachers and students, who were never in my office. They were in classrooms teaching and learning, not just going through the motions.

When I felt a bit down, I'd go observe classes—English, history, science, or whatever, except PE where muscular teachers were brutally torturing weak, frail freshmen. I'd go to an English class and Miss Agnew would still be teaching crazy Emily's poems.

Then I might go to a history class. One time, enthusiastic Mr. Clark was down on his knees in front of a student.

Don't you understand what the Emancipation Proclamation did?

Yes, it was something Nixon wrote about slavery, wasn't it?

Choir classes were my favorite. You don't need an IQ to sing. All a student had to do was open his or her mouth and sing from the heart. The choral teacher was a master. He'd take all kinds of students and blend them into a musical flower garden—all rosebuds, no thorns—and I'd leave feeling replenished and revived.

Maybe I should have occasionally turned on the intercom and announced: Stop everything. We're going to sing "Dream the Impossible Dream." I've done dumber things. The saddest part of educating all the young is that too many give up on their dreams, if they ever had any.

I'd also go to the locker room after the games and compliment the team, and they'd beam. We don't say I'm proud of you enough. I marveled at the athletic, artistic, and academic talents that so many young people have. For those who felt, I can't do anything—and there are many—I tried boosting their confidence.

I believe in you and believe you can do it.

You do?

Would I tell you that if I didn't believe in you?

Perhaps we overemphasize sports and other co-curricular activities, but students who got involved, competed, and participated did better in their classes. At the end of a day, the bell would ring and students went home, except those who stayed for meetings, activities, or practices. They were the happier students. And some had to go to a job to help Mom feed brothers and sisters. I don't know how they did it.

Okay, in a few classes I observed, it was like watching zookeepers feeding the animals, and not all classes were awake. In a few of them, the kids were quiet and dozing, and the teacher was in a trance at his desk. Should I have disturbed them, or let the bell wake them? They were tired and I was, too. I let the bell do it. But those were the exceptions. In all the other classes, kids were learning something worthwhile.

After being uplifted in the choir room, I would head for the office to see who was there, who sent them, and why.

Something was up with a teacher and two students waiting for me. With a wry smile, the teacher said, I found these two in the girl's restroom resting. They haven't been to class yet and it's almost lunchtime. They're yours now; good luck and thanks a lot.

What are your names? With heads down and a whisper—I'm Holly and she's Becky.

Think I'll end this book with a celebration, a birthday celebration. I always celebrate mine in a big way. Some people think birthdays are like every other day, nothing special. I disagree. Every birth is a miracle and each life is, too. Celebrate it.

After that day, I wrote an eighteen-page account, The Celebration of Holly's Birthday. A condensed version follows:

I wiped my temporary warm smile from my face and put on a, you-are-in-big-trouble-frown. Sit down. So you'd rather be in the restroom than in class, huh? I think most males everywhere wonder what females actually do in bathrooms for hours on end.

The two girls hung their heads and stared at the floor. A quick look at their records revealed both had recently enrolled, and were living in the same foster home. They'd been bounced around, from one home this week, and if that didn't work, to another one next week. They were homeless in a sense, and their previous grades and test scores were rock bottom.

Each girl was fifteen and a sophomore. Becky was tall and slender, dressed in a tight black outfit with a wide red belt. She had deep red lips and resembled Bonnie in *Bonnie and Clyde*. Holly was dressed in an attractive blue corduroy suit, and appeared quite mature for her age. She revealed a kind of sweetness and innocence, perhaps like Thelma in the movie *Thelma and Louise*. In my brief initial assessment, it became apparent that both girls had already lived nearly a lifetime in fifteen years.

Neither girl was belligerent or defiant. They were as two little lost lambs bleating for warmth and comfort from the cold. This won't take long.

Tell me why you stayed in the restroom.

We were sick and didn't want to vomit in the classroom or in the hall.

That's what they all say. I'll do my thing, chastise and berate them, then build them back up, and send them on the way.

I could expel you forever, but I'm going to give you a break, I said. Don't go to restrooms, go to classrooms. Learn valuable things from your teachers, then graduate and live happily from this day on. You can't live your life in a restroom. When you get married to raise kids, you will not want your loving husband living in a girl's restroom. Do you want to raise your kids in a restroom or will you want a good home and a good school for them? Grow up.

Experience taught me that you can get the attention of a fifteen-year-old girl if you talk to them about having babies. They do think what it must be like to have a baby, and some of them do.

He's making no sense, so why listen or look at him, look down where we've been, are and will be.

Are you listening to me?

Becky raised her head toward the ceiling. I shouldn't even be here today, she said.

What do you mean, you shouldn't be here today?

My foster mom said I shouldn't be here today. They're sending me to girls' school tomorrow. They don't know what to do with me.

My head dropped down like theirs were. What do I say and do with her—with them? No one says anything until Holly begins tearing up. Handing her a tissue gave me something to do.

I remembered seeing them about a month ago when they came in to enroll—two more foster kids. Don't get too involved with them; they won't be here long. They're temporary because the courts move them around. What is it like, living a temporary life at age fifteen?

Holly was quietly crying—I gave her another tissue—but Becky didn't cry. She gained a bit more confidence in telling me about the plan for the next day. Since she was going to girls' prison for two weeks to be shocked, I realized she knew some things about life I didn't.

I couldn't stay in my office with the two girls all day. Becky, here's what I want you to do. You will go to class, won't you?

Yes.

Do you like our school? Yes.

See you in two weeks. Things will be better then, don't you think?

I don't know what they'll do with me, she said.

Oh, I'll see you in two weeks when you come back. Here's a pass to class.

One down and out and one to go.

I later learned that Becky's mother left home when Becky was a baby. When her father went to prison for murder, she was adopted. Then when her adoptive parents had a child of their own, they no longer wanted Becky. Since that time, she had been unwanted, going from home to home and school to school, running away several times. Was there a place for her, somewhere?

When I gave her the pass, she offered a little smile and said, Thanks. Wish I could issue her a pass to a better life, but who knows? Never saw her again.

Now it was Holly and me, and the tissue box, which was running low. Saying softly, don't cry, only made it worse. I didn't have all day. I could give myself a pass and spend my day in the boys' restroom. What power I had. I could write a pass to send people where I wanted them to go, out of my hair. If only Holly would stop crying, I could send her somewhere.

Holly had Becky to lean on, but now Becky would be gone. Did I want her leaning on me? She might knock me over; I can't do that. Another tissue, wait her out. How many tears can one shed?

Then she said, between sobs, I know she won't come.

What?

I know she won't come.

Who won't come, Holly?

I feel so bad, so bad. I do have trouble, my stomach hurts, my ulcer hurts, she said.

You've got an ulcer?

Since I was six.

What do you say to someone who had an ulcer at six? I had removed my mean face an hour before. Whatever was happening outside my door didn't matter. Between sniffles, Holly began to open up. Her father left her at an early age. Her mother then married an older man, who had a stroke. Holly resented having to care for him. Now her new sister, Becky, had to go to a school for bad girls.

Becky was not a bad girl, she said, and I know she won't come.

Holly, I don't understand. Who won't come?

My mother won't come. She lives a hundred miles away and she's all I have left. Today's my birthday and she's supposed to visit me.

Was she conning me? The hard core can do that. I looked at her record on my desk, and yep, she turned sixteen that day. We sat there until she coughed out: She always bakes a special chocolate cake for me on my birthday.

She does? I would give her another tissue, and she'd give me the soggy one.

Now I was focused on a woman a hundred miles away, who had better come with a cake. How could I get out of this? I said, I'll bet she comes, but don't worry about it; I'll bet she does. Look, you may not realize it, but you have a lot of things going for you. It's wonderful to be young, and you're bright and attractive. Your future can be so promising. Look at it that way. She straightened in her chair, a bit more composed and the tears nearly stopped.

I'm sorry I cry so much, she said.

That's all right. Don't worry about it. Do something for me, will you? I want you to go to class. I'll give you a pass to get yourself together in the restroom, but don't take all day. Then go to class, and I'll call you back later in the day. I want to talk to you again, okay?

Okay.

As she slowly rose from the chair, she said again, I'm sorry I cry so much.

Let me sort this out. She's sorry she cries so much. Becky, her friend and new sister, is going to girls' school tomorrow. Holly will be sitting in class listening to a teacher, but maybe, just maybe, her mind is on her mother or Becky or her birthday or what they'll ever do with her.

It was Holly's sixteenth birthday, and her mother, a hundred miles away, was the only thing she had left, but maybe she wouldn't come with that special chocolate cake.

I had other things to do, stuff building up. I shuffled some papers on my desk, but sat there kind of stunned.

I know what I'll do, I'll go to a store and buy something with chocolate in it, in case that woman doesn't come.

It was lunchtime and I had work to do out in the hallways and the cafeteria where kids were eating like prisoners do. As I moved about chatting, gawking, looking for violations of table manners, I looked for the two girls, but didn't see them. The real world is among the students—the activity, the scurry, the laughter, and pranks, the boundless energy. But there's a raw world inside those who don't know what the system will do with them. They are the ones with no place to go.

Later that afternoon, I sent for Holly. When she came, I left the door slightly ajar. A principal doesn't lock himself in a room alone with a female of any age, and he doesn't give students birthday presents; he'd go broke.

Holly arrived with more composure and confidence, but remained distraught. We began talking amicably, but it didn't take long for the deep emotional trauma to resurface. She was more comfortable with me, but less sure whether her mother would come and she began weeping again.

I know she won't come with that special chocolate cake she always bakes for my birthday. Sorry, I cry when I feel bad. I also cry when people do nice things for me.

She cries when people do nice thing for her. Get it over with. I grabbed the brown paper bag and said, Here Holly, happy birthday.

She slowly pulled out the box of chocolates, and our eyes met for the first time. Where's a tissue when I need one?

Will you hold me, she asked?

We both jumped up and I held her, held her.

God protected me. He did not send anyone to my door to report that Mr. C has a thing going with a sixteen-year-old on her birthday.

She held the paper sack tightly to her chest as she left the room.

Don't open it until you get home, and I'll see you tomorrow.

Early the next day, I just happened to wander down to Holly's first period class. When the bell rang, she came out. It was a bit awkward.

Did your mother come?

Yes.

Did she bring the cake?

Yes.

See, I told you so. She smiled. She glowed.

I walked on down the hall. Five minutes of bedlam, but many more students smiled than frowned or sneered, or blankly stared. Even a few teachers smiled as they stood guard at their door, or welcomed all their students inside. The happiest teachers are those who welcome all their students.

Principals are happy, too, when students say, Hey, Mr. C, how's it going?

It's going good, thank you.

A good school can be judged by its gross happiness quotient, not just the test scores. It is hard, though, to educate those with broken or breaking hearts and dreams. There's a lot of mending to do.

My formal education is over and I can sit back and criticize today's educators like the public does, but it's not as bad as we hear. I have a grandson who is a senior in high school and the past two years, he's taken advanced placement everything. Don't know how he does it. Sixty years ago, I took agriculture, the Kentucky version of the English language, a little government and history, and not that much science or math. The boys also practiced basketball the last period of the day while the girls learned to type. I didn't take books home, because after I helped milk our twenty cows, my mind would go blank.

I have a lot more living to do in the part of my life known as retirement. Retirement does not mean you should completely retire and do nothing. If you did that, your life would be over. I retired from the education profession rather early—partly from burnout—but primarily because

I had too many other things I wanted to do other than persuading teachers and students to remain calm.

Here's a bit of advice for men who retire. Keep your wife working, and then adjust to the tranquility in your house. Dust, wash, and cook for your hard-working wife. There will be plenty of time left over to do what you always wanted to do.

I'm calm now as my second life took off like a rocket ship. I wanted to read, write, run, climb, see the world, contemplate and think. Schoolhouses are not conducive places to think, but that's what we were supposed to teach, isn't it?

I retired on a Monday, and the next Saturday flew halfway around the world to Mt. Everest. In my book, *Retirement is a Blast: Once You Light the Fuse*, I referred to the knots in my stomach when beginning a school day. Somewhere flying over the Artic, I wrote:

Some people get knots in their stomachs at 36,000 feet. I didn't and sat back, totally relaxed, giving my best effort to adjusting to retirement. I felt marvelous floating along above the clouds, in a dream-like trance as the sun began delicately pulling its golden-layered cape from the blue-green earth below. Somewhere over the top of the globe, I eased into the magical presence of a million soft, bright candle-tipped stars. It's not dark up there. You can see through the night and sense a mystical power nudging at your soul. My transformation was complete before the plane touched down.

ACKNOWLEDGEMENTS

Thanks to all the students and teachers who made my life interesting, exciting, and rewarding. And thanks for the times that those students and teachers put my soul to the test. Without a soul, what is there to rely on?

I must also recognize and thank my family and God. Thanks to my family for permitting me to move out of my house into a schoolhouse. Despite the amount of time and attention I gave to my schools, my wife and children did okay, and I'm grateful and proud of them. I'm not sure if God became involved in my daily routine or the writing of this book, but I was blessed with the will and strength that came from a creative source somewhere.

When a writer writes a book, he may think that it could be on a bestseller list. That's before anyone else has read it. When four smart book people waded through my book and provided feedback, I was deeply hurt, but went to work revising it. Many thanks to Cheri Powell, an author and critic, who provided valuable assistance. Robin Baskette, staff member at the Carnegie Center in Lexington, Kentucky, encouraged me to revise the manuscript rather than deleting the whole thing. Kimberly Crum, writing instructor and proprietor of Shape and Flow Writing Studio in Louisville, Kentucky, noted some serious flaws, but indicated there was hope for me. And a very special thanks to my final editor, Susan E. Lindsey.

I used to ask students who their favorite teacher was and why. I remember one student naming Mr. Brown, because "He knows what he's doing." Susan Lindsey knows what she's doing. She's is a writer, editor, and owner of Savvy Communication LLC in Louisville, Kentucky. Susan is a guiding light.

I want to also thank some of my students, who taught me profound things. I pleaded with Freddy to do whatever it takes to pass US history. Take a book to class, stay awake, pretend you're writing stuff down, and you'll get a D-. Don't you want graduate to a bright future? Freddy said he couldn't get interested in history because it was "out of date." He's right. The future is where our lives will be.

ABOUT THE AUTHOR

Terry Cummins was born in the hills of Pendleton County, Kentucky, in the house his great-grandfather built after returning from the Civil War. Terry grew up on this family farm, part of which has been in the family for 145 years. He has a BA from Transylvania University and a MA from the University of Kentucky. After two years in the US Navy, Terry began a career in education: two years as an English teacher and coach followed by thirty-one years in administration, primarily as a high-school principal in Kentucky and Southern Indiana.

After retirement, Terry began a second life following Helen Keller's creed, "Life is an adventure or nothing." His adventures included running marathons, climbing mountains, trekking through many parts of the world, and his compulsion—writing. He ran his first marathon at age sixty-three, climbed his first mountain (20,000 feet) on his sixty-fourth birthday, published his first of over 760 articles at age sixty-six and published the first of six books at age sixty-nine.

Terry has traveled through Siberia and trekked above

the base camp at both the north and south face of Mt. Everest and above base camp at K2. He lived with people in India for a month, climbed mountains in the Andes, and recently hiked through part of Patagonia.

Terry and his wife, Vera, were married more than sixty-one years before she died in 2016. The couple had four children, five grandchildren, and four great-grandchildren who provided a daily dose of pride along with frequent and unexpected surprises.

Other adventures lie ahead and Terry has other articles and books to write.